Entrepreneurial Science

Recent Titles from Quorum Books

Choosing Effective Development Programs: An Appraisal Guide for Human Resources and Training Managers
James Gardner

Investing in Japanese Real Estate
M. A. Hines

Planning, Implementing, and Evaluating Targeted Communication Programs: A Manual for Business Communicators
Gary W. Selnow and William D. Crano

The United States Trade Deficit of the 1980s: Origins, Meanings, and Policy Responses
Chris C. Carvounis

The Legal Handbook of Business Transactions: A Guide for Managers and Entrepreneurs
E. C. Lashbrooke, Jr., and Michael I. Swygert

Federal Statutes on Environmental Protection: Regulation in the Public Interest
Warren Freedman

The Marketer's Guide to Media Vehicles, Methods, and Options: A Sourcebook in Advertising and Promotion
Ann Grossman

Corporate Asset Management: A Guide for Financial and Accounting Professionals
Clark E. Chastain

The Control of Municipal Budgets: Toward the Effective Design of Tax and Expenditure Limitations
David Merriman

Business Strategy and Public Policy: Perspectives from Industry and Academia
Alfred A. Marcus, Allen M. Kaufman, and David R. Beam, editors

Professional Sports and Antitrust
Warren Freedman

Office Systems Integration: A Decision-Maker's Guide to Systems Planning and Implementation
Barbara S. Fischer

ENTREPRENEURIAL SCIENCE *NEW LINKS BETWEEN CORPORATIONS, UNIVERSITIES, AND GOVERNMENT*

Robert F. Johnston
and
Christopher G. Edwards

QUORUM BOOKS

NEW YORK
WESTPORT, CONNECTICUT
LONDON

Library of Congress Cataloging-in-Publication Data

Johnston, Robert F.
  Entrepreneurial science.

  Bibliography: p.
  Includes index.
  1. High technology industries—United States.
2. Research, Industrial—United States. 3. Industry
and education—United States. 4. Universities and
colleges—United States—Graduate work. 5. Research
and development contracts, Government—United States.
I. Edwards, Christopher G. II. Title.
HC110.H53E39   1987   338′.06   87-2518
ISBN 0-89930-260-2 (lib. bdg. : alk. paper)

Library of Congress Catalog Card Number: 87-2518
ISBN: 0-89930-260-2

First published in 1987 by Quorum Books

Greenwood Press, Inc.
88 Post Road West, Westport, Connecticut 06881

Printed in the United States of America

The paper used in this book complies with the
Permanent Paper Standard issued by the National
Information Standards Organization (Z39.48-1984).

10 9 8 7 6 5 4 3 2 1

Contents

1. Technology 2000: An Overview   1

2. The Biotechnology Company: An Entrepreneurial Pattern   7

3. Large Companies Look to the University   21

4. The Universities: Allies with Industry   29

5. Federal and State Assistance for High Technology   49

6. Pro-competitive Research: A New Way to Do Business   71

7. The Technology Transfer Specialists   81

8. The Financing of New Ventures   95

9. The Research and Development Limited
   Partnership: Potentials and Problems   103

10. Government Strategies in R&D: A Comparison   115

11. Some Implications   127

12. A View of the Future   133

   Notes   139

   Bibliography   141

   Index   147

Entrepreneurial Science

1   Technology 2000: An Overview

A dramatic revolution is taking place in the American economy, a transformation that will force you to make difficult and risky decisions now if you want to be successful in the year 2000. If you expect that money, excitement and intellectual challenge will follow your career in a large corporation, the chances are great that you're dead wrong. If you believe that you will be surrounded by the best and the brightest colleagues in management or research as you climb your way to the top of the corporate ladder in a large company, you're wrong again. If you're betting your career, your living conditions, and the environment for your family on the hope that you will reap far greater financial rewards near the top of the ladder than your colleagues who start their own businesses, you're wrong again.

Small business, once derided by executives as Mom and Pop shops, will be the key to the expansion of the U.S. economy in the year 2000, offering all of the excitement, independence, financial rewards and challenges that you can expect in your career. The money, talented people and resources are already flowing away from large corporations into startups. The key to this drastic shift in the economy is the explosion of high technology opportunities based upon research conducted at universities. Biotechnology, computer hardware and software, laser and optical technologies, and robotics have already formed major tributaries in the river of money that flows throughout the economy.

Expect that by the year 2000 the power of the economy will be in the hands of companies that specialize in transforming scientific research into technology and products. Large corporations will be the marketing, manufacturing and financing machines, buying equity, research contracts and marketing rights from smaller companies. The high-technology companies will form a new, dominant corporate class in the economy. Nested comfortably between the universities and the larger corporations, they will be the essential link between research and development. Large corporations currently spend about 2 to 3 percent of their research budgets on research and development contracts with high technology companies. These companies will devote 40 percent or more of their research budgets to contracts with the high-tech firms in the year 2000.

Expect that high technology will be America's economic panacea, saving it from the types of losses suffered by countries like England and France during earlier industrial revolutions. Just as industrial technology lifted West Germany and Japan out of the ashes of World War II and into the league of the super powers, the next stage of the post-industrial economy will determine tomorrow's leaders. America has a chance to surpass its current position in the world economy if it heeds the characteristics of the new economy: rapidly growing and shifting markets, flexible manufacturing systems, dramatic cost-cutting in manufacturing, and the ability to quickly develop new industrial and consumer products that will render competitors' products obsolete. America is already unable to compete with other countries in the areas of natural resource exploration and labor-intensive manufacturing. Given the relatively high cost of labor in the United States and the scientific, financial and entrepreneurial advantages in this country, high technology will be the hope of the coming decades for American business.

High technology depends upon the explosion of scientific knowledge that has already launched major new industries, a trend that will almost certainly increase. Because of breakthroughs in more basic levels of scientific research (primarily at the level of the cell and the atom) and the development of new manufacturing technologies, the speed of commercialization from the lab bench to the factory has accelerated rapidly. This makes it more attractive for universities and research companies to work together more closely, exchanging research talent and results for money and commercial direction. Expect this trend to accelerate, enriching those universities with the foresight to acknowledge that corporate funding must replace the rapidly shrinking government research dollar. As the undisputed world leader in most areas of scientific research, the United States will mine this resource through the high-technology company.

As the high-technology company receives the attention that it deserves, expect that it will increase in attractiveness for many of the brightest young business executives and scientists, drawing talent away from the large corporation and, to a lesser extent, the university. The advantages of the high-tech company for the upwardly mobile executive will prove too great to resist. It is the fastest and easiest way to make money, potentially offering rewards in equity that are hundreds of times greater than what larger companies are willing to offer. The entrepreneurial company offers a more personal and hospitable environment where the executive can achieve quicker and more direct results compared to his or her alternative in the middle of a corporate pyramid. Once it becomes clear that many new opportunities exist for middle managers to leave large companies to build high-tech firms, thousands of talented executives will make this move each year, many occupying the president's chairs in the new firms.

Intrapreneuring, the trend among some giant corporations to keep their best talent by simulating a startup atmosphere, will fail over the next fifteen years. Although it will provide some of the needed innovation for large corporations, it won't keep the talent from migrating to the startups. This is because large corporations are unwilling to offer the higher rewards of stock options and the greater independence offered by the startups. Intrapreneurial divisions will never provide the opportunities for executives to be their own bosses. Finally, since intrapreneurial efforts are conducted to meet the product development needs of the large corporation, they will pass up many of the great opportunities that small companies will grab: opportunities to develop products that need quick development for small market segments. This is because the large corporation, when compared to the small startup, is a lumbering giant: it spends too much money for its survival and moves too slowly since it must support a vast bureaucracy.

The investment banking industry in the year 2000 should be in good condition, but executives will not fare so well if they do not begin now to acknowledge and shift toward the area where investments will flow, the high-tech corporation. According to the capitalist equation, money begets money. If most of today's trends continue as expected, there will be far more money available through financial institutions to give high-tech startups the push they need to get started. As the economy expands, investors have more excess money and a greater willingness to gamble intelligently on the riskier, higher stakes of the high-tech company. This money will be available through the rapidly expanding field of venture capitalism and through large investment banks. The venture capitalists are acquiring better skills to assess new technologies. Because of their continuing success and the confidence it breeds, they can attract more money from private and institutional investors. The large investment banks have created financing mechanisms that allow them to pool investments into high-tech firms through portfolios. This gives them the ability to attract large investors and give the rates of return at risk ratios that are tolerable for the larger corporate investor.

In addition to the flood of capital from domestic financial institutions, high-tech companies will enjoy an influx of foreign money that will undoubtedly expand over the next fifteen years. This money is crossing the waters because the United States is developing an economy with the right set of ingredients for high-tech startups to flourish. The prime ingredients include: superior scientific manpower; an emerging entrepreneurial class of executives for high-tech enterprises; a university system that is growing more receptive each year to corporate dollars; large corporations that can provide additional financial and marketing clout; and a venture capital industry that can help foreign investors spot the right new technologies and cut the right deals.

How are large corporations adapting to the insight that high-tech companies are the key to the economy's future? They are expanding their base of research and technology in several ways: they are nurturing entrepreneurial high-tech firms, both as investments and as windows on technology; they are providing substantial support toward boosting the level and amount of scientific research conducted at universities; large corporations that competed fiercely for decades are banding together to form hugh research and technology cooperatives where some of their best scientists and engineers work side by side; they are adjusting their in-house product development capabilities to complement the technology that they buy from high-technology corporations; large corporations are lobbying in Washington for legislation that would expand university-based scientific research, protect domestic corporations from patent infringement by foreign competitors, and ease the commercialization of technology in this country; and major corporations are starting or expanding their own venture capital divisions, branches of the companies that make corporate investment in high-risk, high-return technology-based startups.

As corporate awareness increases, the federal government has grown to recognize that high technology is the heart of the economy for the year 2000 and beyond. It is legislating this future in many ways. For example, it is making available a vast reservoir of government-supported research for commercialization by pioneers in high technology. It is also organizing entire industries to voluntarily pursue cooperative research and development to stave off Japanese and European threats to the economy. The federal government has changed the tax laws to favor investment in high technology research, and there is evidence that this trend will accelerate.

All of the trends toward the high technology future dictate that the savvy executive pay attention and plan his or her career to meet the demands of the economy in the year 2000. The following chapters provide the information that any executive would need to understand these movements, predict the probable future, and go for it.

2 The Biotechnology Company: An Entrepreneurial Pattern

Biotechnology companies form an important new pattern for high technologies flowing out of universities and into specialty companies. Biotechnology had the right combination of risk, commercial potential, and novelty to attract venture capital as venture capital became increasingly available in the late 1970's and early 1980's. When we look at biotechnology we see a pattern that might be applicable in following other new technologies.

One important characteristic of biotechnology is the very short lead time from discovery to application. A laboratory finding can, in many cases, lead to a path of product development almost immediately after the finding is published. This is the reason why universities and biotech companies almost universally insist on a review of patentability of the finding before actually publishing the result. The short lead time makes it important for scientists in biotech firms to be close to university scientists. In some cases the biotech firm is contracting to the university, giving the company all the proprietary rights to the discovery-turned-invention. The scientists stand to benefit from these types of associations; they can make money for themselves or their department while advancing knowledge in such a way that their peers in other universities respect the originality and importance of their findings.

The technology of biotechnology is solid, another characteristic which lends itself to commercialization through the specialty company. Although it is a new enough field to lend itself to speculation, it is based upon a flood of basic research at the cellular level that uncovered secrets of how genes operate in cells and how genes can be altered by scientists. The solidity and wide-ranging nature of these fundamental scientific findings make biotechnology an important investment for large corporations and bankers who specialize in new ventures. These large corporations and bankers see great flexibility in the structure of the biotechnology company. Universities also realize that the specialty company can be flexible, working in tandem with the universities.

One advantage of the small specialty firm is that the entire corporation can focus upon a small number of promising products. The products are likely to receive greater attention than they would if they were being developed by established companies. This phenomenon also allows companies to take on products that might be passed up by the large corporation because the markets are too small to justify the product development. In addition, the larger companies don't have the scientific talent to commercialize their biotechnology products. They have to rely on smaller companies who can develop the product faster and more easily. For example, when Johnson & Johnson saw the biotech race heat up, it developed good research relations with the Scripps Institute and started Biotech Inc., a small biotechnology company a few blocks away from the Institute. When compared with the large corporation, small companies can move more quickly with the superior scientific staff they have assembled. It is well known that large companies are adverse to risks. It is to their advantage to push along the entrepreneurial company, allowing it to absorb the risk of failure. This enables the large company to retain what it does best—manage large budgets and pour its resources into manufacturing and selling large amounts of products.

The entrepreneurial company often begins with an idea in the mind of a principal investor. At Johnston Associates, for example, venture capitalists go to the technical meetings and accept invitations to visit university labs to learn of the most promising findings. There is a rare mix here of higher-level scientific communication and specialty in financing. Both parties soon learn how to communicate from their disciplines. Negotiations usually proceed between the principal investigator of the project and the venture capitalist. The scientist might be offered product royalties, equity in the company or financial support to the department through the university administration. Scientists who a few years ago were gun-shy now welcome the investment; the traditional barricades between business and academia have broken down in these fields forever. Depending upon university regulations, the principal investigator might arrange to have some of the work done in his laboratories or he would agree to work on a part-time basis at private labs that would be built conveniently off-campus. Once an agreement is made between the principal investigator and the venture capitalist, the next step is to obtain the blessings of the administration for certain aspects of the deal.

Once agreements are made with the scientist, it is important that the investment of the venture capitalist's money is secure. Solid management must be found. Management of the specialty company begins with a board of directors composed of representatives of the investors.

Excellent science and technology are useless to a company that can't form work teams and carefully organize the technology with the financing and marketing functions. Good CEOs are sought, people who are entrepreneurial enough to take the risk of failure and are well-seasoned enough to meet the challenge of starting a company. In biotechnology, there has been a shaking out of executives. Today you are more likely to see the position of CEO taken by someone who has had ten or more years of experience in developing technology for the chemical, pharmaceutical, or agricultural industries. In addition to a reasonably competitive salary, the biotech firm can offer substantial equity, a satisfactory enticement for the successful executive.

It is instructive to see how some of these companies make use of their managerial talents. BioTechnica, a Boston-based biotechnology company, has carved out a role for itself as a company that first concentrates on contract research while building subsidiary and associate companies that can offer equity to scientists and management. It employs consultants at universities who operate at approximately the same level as their in-house scientists. This allows an intellectual technology transfer to take place. According to its former president and current deputy chairman, Ralph Hardy, it has relations with the Forsyth Dental Center for research on bacteria involved with periodontal disease. Lynn Klotz, vice president, claims that the company has completed 95 percent of the research and launched the product, using DNA probes to detect diseases caused by different microorganisms. BioTechnica also has a joint research venture in England involving fermentation of waste products, BioTechnica Limited. The strategy is to establish companies in defined entrepreneurial areas which have technical skills that complement but do not duplicate BioTechnica's recombinant DNA molecular biology capabilities. For example, the English company's technical skills have to do with natural communities of microorganisms that turn garbage dumps into methane. Its strength is in microbial ecology. The company can supply genes from bacteria that can be used by BioTechnica in herbicides and pesticides. By setting up subsidiaries, Klotz remarks, "you retain that kind of freshness and entrepreneurial aspect that got a lot of scientists diving out of laboratories" several years ago.

Does the strategy of setting up affiliate companies diffuse the technical resources of the company? Klotz denies that there is significant diffusion, stating that each affiliate has its own independent group of researchers working on their own accounts. "Of course we're all tied together through contracts and equity exchange so they truly are related companies. Whether that's a good or bad strategy, time will tell." There is some diffusion in that involvement in these subsidiaries takes time out of management. Although they're independent entities, they are coordinated through joint arrangements and sharing of board positions, so they take the attention and the time of management away from internal affairs. "That's the one area where you might worry that such a strategy could be detrimental to the core company, the parent company," states Klotz.

The English establishment began about a year after BioTechnica was first being funded. The English company received its funding elsewhere, yet there was great interest on the part of BioTechnica in setting up a European presence. BioTechnica ended up owning a sizeable portion of the English company's stock, 32 percent.

The dental company started under different circumstances. BioTechnica wanted to attract high-level employees with equity offers. The company had been around too long to have substantial amounts of equity available for new researchers and new management. The Forsyth Dental Center was interested at the same time in forming a working relationship with BioTechnica, so a deal was made. Forsyth brings technical expertise to the new venture and owns a minor equity position. BioTechnica contributes its patent rights to some of the research begun there. Forsyth supplies consultants and microbial cultures for the research. It will also conduct some of the clinical trials for products coming out of BioTechnica Diagnostics. Klotz has a staff of twenty-five there. He admits that BioTechnica's strategy of forming affiliates and subsidiaries happened almost by accident; these two opportunities came at the right time, and the affiliate format was the way to go.

It is too early to tell whether the affiliates strategy will work. The answers will come in the marketplace, where BioTechnica may have to compete with the large, established firms. Klotz suggests that the success or failure of their strategy will become more apparent in about three years. He is open to the possibility that BioTechnica, like many other biotechnology companies, might become a target for acquisition. This may come about because of marketplace realities, not because of technological leadership, which the biotechnology companies will retain.

We honestly do not discuss whether we can get somebody to buy us out, because we really want to get as far as we can on our own. However, in the back of their minds most people realize that things might get too tough out there at some point. We had better anticipate that, because if you don't anticipate it your value might go down. If you're on the verge of going broke and you try to sell yourself, you're not going to get a good deal.

BioTechnica is doing well so far under the leadership of Ralph Hardy. Hardy was recruited from academia into DuPont where he worked for twenty years, finally becoming director of life sciences research there. He left DuPont to become president of BioTechnica, where he now serves as deputy chairman. In addition to this, he keeps one foot in academia, serving as a visiting professor at Cornell University. Hardy is pleased with the talent he can tap.

The technical quality of this organization is overall superbly better than say DuPont's quality. Part of it is the community. Harvard's a couple of miles away, MIT's close by, so we have tapped in very effectively from that. It's Boston, not Wilmington, Delaware. It's small, it's a startup, and there's equity for the scientists. . . . Everybody, when the company succeeds, can clearly see their own bottom line; they look at their number of shares, and there's real interest. [The company is] small enough so that they can understand it, can relate to it and feel they can make a major impact. Any one individual can make a significant impact upon the company. The scientists at DuPont were driven by peer recognition and very little of what it will do for the corporation.

Hardy feels that companies like DuPont cannot accomplish technology transfer like the specialty companies because there is no pull on technology from marketing. The conservative atmosphere in marketing in large corporations exists because it is safer to stick with known products with assurance of high profits; nobody likes to be caught with a failure. Hardy asks:

How do you mobilize an organization to effectively create a climate to encourage technology transfer? I think the way to do it is to create marketing positions for individuals who have very little in their market basket. And they have to be aggressively looking for things to put in their market basket but they must understand that there will be some failures out of it and they and management must accept that fact. Have those individuals report in at an appropriate level of the organization so they have the ability to make those decisions. So you're going to have people pull on the technology.

Hardy's a firm believer that established corporations are going to have to find a way to more effectively decentralize if they are going to compete, develop leadership as opposed to management skills, and have individuals take risks without the excessive reviewing structure, "so that they create entrepreneurial pockets or a multiplicity of entrepreneurial activity and the management is really there as a resource to help facilitate these people as opposed to objecting."

Hardy, who is also a member of the National Research Council, views the new ties forming between government, industry, and the university as a form of experiment. "If the experiment's a bad one it won't be repeated. I think that out of this more daring, adventuresome period the universities will evolve some new ways of doing things." Hardy explains that the university, government, and industry will maintain their traditional roles, but the way these three institutions relate to one another will change. "And it will probably be promoted most by people fluxing between them." He believes that this change will make the United States economy more competitive.

Regardless of the results of this experiment, biotechnology companies will not compete with universities in doing basic research or with large corporations for manufacturing and marketing power. The basic question these companies must ask is how they, with superior applied research capabilities as their strength can fit between these organizations.

The problem is particularly acute in biotechnology because many of the products must pass through the slow and extremely expensive route of Food and Drug Administration approval. At this stage, some biotech companies are very conservative in their new product development because their resources are strained by what they are already working on. With only so much money, how can that money be properly spent to assure a good cash flow in the present as well as a future of new products? When research directors and chief executives at several of these companies were interviewed recently, they presented a sober view of the future of these companies. By making manufacturing and marketing agreements with large corporations, they can ease the financial strain while excluding themselves from some of the big profits that the products are likely to make. As long as these types of agreements are made, there is less impetus for the large corporation to boost its in-house capabilities; it can simply buy the technology from the small companies.

The fate of the small company's product begins with the applied research. The research is largely conducted by former professors and young graduates recruited from molecular biology and biochemistry programs at universities. The market for such talent seems to have stabilized. There appear to be enough good graduates with interest in biotech companies. Although equity offers are not available in many cases, the company can still offer attractive salary and benefits as well as a congenial, university-like atmosphere. Senior scientists in the companies often know the new recruits, making the sale a bit easier. Finally, grad students often learn about the company through shared research projects that may involve university and corporate researchers and take place in university labs. In some cases the grad student goes to the corporation to work with a senior scientist like the student who follows his professor to another university for grad school.

The biotech companies do not have the type of image problem that large corporations often have with students. Biotechnology is entrepreneurial, with an emphasis on independence and creativity. Many of the grad students available now grew up during a time of rebellion in the 1960's and early 1970's; they may not have been radical students, but they picked up some of the values of that generation. The large corporations have the reputation of being slow and extremely bureaucratic, exchanging creativity for seniority. In the biotech company, the student expects to make a niche for himself. Because of the small size of the biotech company, the researcher can gain a reputation in the company more easily. In summary, choosing to go to a biotech company rather than a giant corporation is partly a choice of life-style. As long as the biotech companies continue to do good research, they will have the edge over the large corporation when recruiting students.

There is still some controversy about how dependent the specialty companies are upon the university. According to J. Leslie Glick, former president of Genex Corporation, his company never depended heavily upon the universities as a source of research. He claims that Genex proved that it could do the basic research necessary for product development as soon as the company decided it should be done. Glick believes that biotech's dependence upon the university is greatly overemphasized.

At the other end of the spectrum is Centocor, a very successful biopharmaceutical company that has always emphasized strong dependence upon universities and non-profit research institutes for development of its diagnostic products. It focuses upon genetic engineering and monoclonal antibody technologies. One key to the company's success has been its strategy of making numerous deals with universities, investors, and distributors. Chairman Michael Wall explains that Centocor's product development centers around joint ventures for work conducted at fifteen separate research institutions including the Massachusetts General Hospital, Tianjin Cancer Institute in China, and the Max-Planck Institute in Germany. The company also has numerous marketing agreements with companies such as Hoffman-La Roche, FMC Corporation, and Warner-Lambert.

One form of financing the company has used is the limited partnership. The first one was formed in 1984, Centocor Oncogene Research Partners, to identify specific oncogenes associated with specific cancers and to use oncogene proteins in diagnostic tests. This research and development limited partnership (RDLP) brought in $5 million. The company next raised $23.1 million from investors for Centocor Cardiovascular Imaging Partners, L.P. (CCIP). This limited partnership covers the research, development, and human clinical testing of Anti-Myosin and Anti-Fibrin, two imaging agents that can be used in diagnosing various cardiovascular diseases. There is no obligation for pay back if the products fail. If they succeed, the company pays a 7 percent royalty. In both partnerships, the company has the option to buy back the rights to the technology which were assigned to the limited partnership in the agreement. Centocor has recently bought back the rights for the technology from Oncogene Research Partners. The company recently formed a joint venture agreement with CCIP to the manufacture, market, and sublicense to third parties the manufacture, use and sale of any products within CCIP's field of activity. The joint venture also covers an agreement with a new European center for Centocor, Centocor Europe B.V. (CEBV), to manufacture and market the joint venture's products. CEBV will eventually be the production facility for the company's in vivo products.

Established in 1979, Centocor had 1985 revenues of $22.4 million with product sales of $7 million. Hambrecht & Quist estimates that Centocor will pass the $50 million revenue mark next year and that more than half of the revenues will be derived from product sales. It estimates that from 1987 onward, Centocor will move rapidly toward $100 million in revenues, which it could achieve in 1988 and certainly will in 1989. A publicly traded company, it also issued one million shares of common stock in a public offering on December 20, 1985. In addition to its other agreements, Centocor has a joint venture with FMC called Immunorex Associates, which aims to produce large quantities of human antibodies and perform research in immunoregulation.

Centocor has rapidly moved to establish itself as an international company. The presence of CEBV, the numerous research contracts distributed internationally, and the sale of 75 percent of its products in 1985 to foreign markets attest to this fact. The company has also moved closer to its goal of having therapeutic products as its core business, even though it has been dependent upon the sale of diagnostic products for much of its income so far. This is all part of the company's strategy. Its marketing strategy includes using proceeds from the sale of its stock to purchase an equity interest in Dianon, Inc., a marketing company which has clinical oncologists as its marketing target. This is important for Centocor because a large part of its product development is for diagnosis and treatment of cancer. This purchase may be related to the company's desire to have its own sales force for its in vivo therapeutic products.

Three therapeutic products are being tested. One is a monoclonal antibody for the treatment of colorectal cancer, which is in Phase II clinical trials in the United States. Another new product will be a human antibody that treats Gram-negative infections, bacterial infections resulting from endotoxins released by bacteria into the blood in burn patients and patients who have undergone surgery. In the future, Centocor will continue to test a monoclonal antibody for the treatment of blood clotting found with various cardiovascular diseases.

Michael Wall explains his strategy for selecting a potential product: "The rules that we have are that the product must be unique and well ahead of the competition. The product must have a market of at least $30 million. And third, the market must at least have the potential for accepting the product rapidly. The company is unusual in not relying on any sales force for its diagnostic products. It specializes in finding the right large corporation to purchase its antibodies to incorporate in their products or product line."

The company is so dependent upon university technology that it doesn't have its own research director. "If I hire a research director, he'll want to do the research," Wall explains. Instead, Centocor relies upon finding the right research to fund, something that a large corporation wouldn't touch because it would prefer to develop it in-house. Wall believes that for this reason there is no competition between what he does and what the large corporation wants to do. The company does do some product development in-house, however—about $9 million worth in 1985. Centocor is a company which investors in biotechnology should follow. By licensing technology outside of its main product focus, it has been able to work consistently toward its product goals. Expect Centocor to be a leader in its field in the 1990's.

There are other types of arrangements with universities, for example the one started by Engenics, another specialty company, with an unusual type of agreement with the University of California and Stanford. The company was started by faculty members at those universities to do work on process development. They received initial support from Bendix, Elf Aquitaine, Mead, Koppers, General Foods and Noranda. In addition, the investors have started the non-profit Center for Biotechnology Research (CBR), which funnels research money into the university labs. These projects can then be picked up and commercialized by Engenics. Engenics understands itself to be a bioprocess technology organization for the investors, even though it acts like other companies in seeking contracts for process development from other large corporations. Instead of selling products it sells engineering methodology to its customers and funnels its results directly to its investors.

Why did the group of companies found Engenics? According to the president, John Richardson,

I think the question again goes back to one of timing and maybe not knowing what was required, not having it in-house, having it obviously for any individual company be a high risk to totally develop it itself, and to not really have its own product direction all that well defined. So Engenics came into being. . . . I think that it basically comes down to the issue of our minimizing their risk and we minimize their risk by doing things that we're good at that they are not well positioned to do and that they can't see others that readily able to do as well . . . minimizing the risk, avoiding the capital investment, avoiding the extra expense of hiring specialty staff for an unknown period.

They have the benefits of some of the best minds at the University of California for this venture capital investment.

How does the technology finally get transferred from the biotech company to the large corporation? The specialty company can sell the manufacturing and marketing rights without revealing proprietary information concerning the technology's development. Although a great deal must be revealed to a potential manufacturer, patent protection and secrecy agreements can help prevent a cooperative concern from becoming a competitor. The question is: how do you give away just enough technology to manufacture the product and nothing more?

Biotech companies have to remember not to be overly dependent upon these corporate sources of manufacturing and marketing. Genex Corporation learned this the hard way. After purchasing a factory and gearing up to manufacture large quantities of aspartame under contract to G. D. Searle Corp., Searle refused to renew the agreement, which accounted for 83 percent of Genex's total revenues in 1985. The debacle which followed involved the dismissal of 40 percent of the company's employees and the restructuring of the company so that it would primarily do contract research for large corporations.

The strategy in biotech is for the specialty company to make use of the power of a large corporation without succumbing to it. This means that the company must go to the table knowing exactly what it wants to get out of the relationship. Promises are not enough. In the case of Genex, it had every reason to believe that the contract would be renewed.

Expect that contract research will decline in the next few years. Contract research occurs when the corporation doesn't have the time or the expertise to perform the research itself. Large corporations are expanding their research facilities to a point where they may be able to do the research in-house in a cost-effective way. Biotech companies would like to avoid the situation where their immediate revenues dry up while a key product is still in the manufacturing or early marketing stages. There will probably always be room for some contract research. This dependence upon the large corporation for research revenues underscores the interdependence of biotech companies with established firms.

What happens when biotech companies stretch their financing too much in order to attempt to remain independent? Lubrizol's purchase of an overextended Agrigenetics may be a good example of what many specialty companies will experience. Lubrizol started its examination of opportunities in 1977, taking an equity stake in Genentech, where they are supporting a research project. Since Lubrizol is in the oils business, they were interested in genetic modification of oil seed crops, specifically the sunflower and grape seed. The company acquired a seed research company, then started up a genetic engineering company, buying 25 percent equity in Sungene Technology. When they decided to expand their technology base and apply it to conventional commodity crops, they heard about Agrigenetics, a promising company that was deeply in debt. Agrigenetics is now operating as a subsidiary company which intends to be fully integrated into manufacturing and sales. In the area of modified oil seed crops, it will operate differently: Agrigenetics will do the planting and breeding for Lubrizol, then sell it or otherwise transfer it to another Lubrizol company for production and sales. Lubrizol, in addition, will continue its policy of funding university laboratories for applied research programs and will deepen its investment in biotech. It recently invested in Creative Biomolecules and Mycogen.

Will the biotech company of the future be caught in the middle, between the university and the large corporation, or will it tend to integrate into a manufacturing and marketing company? The odds are good that many of these companies won't grow enough to become fully integrated. Some will undoubtedly share the fate of Agrigenetics and be purchased for use by the larger, established corporations, but there is plenty of room in the middle. There is room for a company to grow with both research and technology development without ever integrating. The biotech company now occupies a unique niche. It is filling a place where the multinationals don't want to be because of the high risk and, in some cases, the relatively small markets. The biotech company can be medium-sized and still provide the perks for the scientists that it provides now. This would not be the case for the company that sold out to an Eli Lilly or a Monsanto.

There ought to be more companies like Centocor, with the courage to select pockets of technology at the university and commercialize them directly. There should be more funding schemes to be relied upon besides the R&D limited partnership, which has fallen out of favor in biotech because of changes in the tastes of investors. There's room for more new companies which can interact easily with university professors, finding research in the engineering colleges like Georgia Tech where professors are eager to get funded. All it takes is some entrepreneurial vision and sharp analysis with the funding to back them up.

How can we learn from the biotechnology companies? Is it a pattern to be imitated in other high-tech areas? The answer is not clear. There are certain areas of software engineering, especially artificial intelligence, that have a similar balance between the academic and corporate spheres. The venture capital community has the capacity to support new industries emerging from academia. The real criterion to look for is how thin a line exists between basic research and product development. In biotech, that line is fortunately very thin, allowing companies to be creative in their relations with the universities and the large corporations.

3   Large Companies Look to
the University

Many of the leaders in biotechnology don't expect to survive without
the help of universities. Here and in other selected technologies, the
large corporations have seen the wisdom of becoming close allies with
universities. In some cases a relationship with a university may be
more fruitful than working with a specialty company. In other cases,
it supplements a policy that makes various attempts to transfer fresh
technology into the manufacturing stage. A relationship with a university helps establish the window on new technology, giving clues that
will help the industrial scientist in his work. In one study of fifty-six
companies conducted by Peters and Fusfeld at NYU's Center for Science and Technology Policy, the authors concluded that "access to
high quality manpower is the prime motivation underlying industry's
desire to establish joint university/industry research programs." [1] Peters and Fusfeld report that when Exxon became concerned about the
manpower crisis in its field, it announced a $15 million grant program
to support graduate fellows and supplement faculty salaries at sixty-
six institutions.

The grants to departments or professors usually follow a period of
courtship between the university and the corporation. In some cases
the alliance centers around a piece of technology that the company
wants to commercialize. In many cases, however, the company is not
as interested in the technology as in the relationship to the professor,
a source of young talent from the graduating students and a source for
consulting by the professor. Motorola's E. David Metz claims that
university relations "is a plus in the recruiting effort, there's no question about it. And that is a key effort in much of our university rela-

tions." This is also why companies are so willing to donate equipment. There is an additional motive here: companies want these purchasers of equipment to get accustomed to using and ordering supplies from the sponsoring company. The informal contacts between university and industrial scientists are very important. They are allies, not competitors, with a mutual interest in seeing the basic research and technology grow.

Why is consulting important in these relationships? The corporation does not look for engineering know-how. It looks for basic understanding of processes. Motorola's Metz explains: "Very often [the consultant] catalyzes within the company—if it's a strong company— the already existing pockets of knowledge and understanding and a willingness to take a new approach which some of them might have thought of already, but were either unwilling or unable to make happen."

The universities have become more receptive to associations with industry as the federal monies for research have diminished. At some universities you see professors using their sabbatical time to work in industry as consultants and lecturers. You can also find industrial internships for the students and, in some cases, paid fellowships. In biotechnology there is not much question about the sincerity of the industrial partners or their desire to allow the faculty member his freedom to teach and publish as he desires. Most universities who have industrial contacts have worked out a policy which prevents professors from giving up their teaching or research time to help the corporation. Although it would be wise to look at each university policy in detail, it can be said that the policy usually allows the professor a percentage of his time for these off-campus pursuits. It may forbid the use of graduate students for industrial projects and it usually has some ruling regarding the use of laboratory space. It may also have worked out fees for consulting—either a restriction on fees or possibly a fee-sharing policy with the university is determined. The university policy also varies with the branch of the company funding the projects. The operating division of a company may want to sponsor a series of narrow and highly secretive agreements, responding to short-term goals; in contrast, the company's foundation or corporate headquarters would be likely to offer money with few or no expectations about commercializing the research.

While biotech grows on this university foundation of knowledge the semiconductor companies have just recently turned to the universities for help. In the very early days of biotechnology, it was possible to start a company with a general business plan and a list of highly esteemed professors. The technology is still very dependent upon university research. Any large corporation trying to get along in biotech without a university alliance will have great difficulty. The semiconductor industry, mature by biotech's standards, is now showing great interest in sponsoring university research. This is a result of the competition that the Japanese have demonstrated in their field and the ambitious plans for Japanese domination. The origins of the industry help explain the tardiness in establishing university ties. The semiconductor industry sprang up in California and Boston through government contracts to small private companies. Computers did not play such a great role in university research then. All of the R&D was conducted in-house with industrial scientists. Before the Japanese challenge, competition in the field was limited enough for this situation to continue. Now, however, semiconductor companies are funding large programs at Stanford, MIT, Cornell and various other campuses to strengthen the basic research component. Support can come from the corporate foundation, the company's central laboratories, divisional laboratories, or operating units which manufacture and distribute products. In microelectronics, as in other fields, it is most likely to come from corporate research laboratories.

In biotechnology some of the deals made with universities include staggering amounts of money. Monsanto, for example, has promised $23.5 million to Washington University over five years to fund research projects there on proteins and peptides. The projects are determined by a committee composed of scientists from both institutions. The faculty is free to publish after patent reviews are made. There is a significant secrecy clause in the agreement: until Monsanto approves a publication, secrecy must remain for two years with an additional option to renew for two years. Faculty members submit their proposals for research as if they were applying for a grant. Royalties for any product will go to the university, not the researcher, and Monsanto will obtain an exclusive license for all work. The deal does not prohibit the Washington University faculty from conducting any research sponsored by the government or any other company.

Edward MacCordy, Associate Vice Chancellor for Research, views the agreement as a creative one for both faculty and the corporation.

"The ideas for new projects are popping up daily in people's minds all over the medical school. . . . It's a maximum access to the creative ideas and research in a university setting." He emphasizes the breadth of the agreement:

The beauty of this agreement is in that it is not focused on a single or a narrow aspect of the company. Instead, what a company sponsor does in something like this is to say "here, I'm going to establish a fund." That fund, number one, will not be restricted to a single laboratory or single investigator but will be available to anybody and everybody in that institution who has good researchable ideas that fit within the broad areas of interest of the company.

Monsanto has supported about thirty projects so far, spending about $12 million. The first patent was recently issued, a project of Philip Needleman for peptides that affect blood pressure. It is understood that Washington University scientists will not be involved in product development. Furthermore, they will not receive any income from the resulting inventions. Income will flow back into the laboratory, department, or medical school to fund additional research. In fact, Washington University has the unusual policy of not allowing their faculty members to accept income beyond their salaries.

Monsanto has the right of first refusal on all inventions and screens all publications for possible patentable inventions.

Part of the beauty of the arrangement is that it coexists with other funding mechanisms, such as National Institutes of Health grants. Says MacCordy, "there's absolutely no compulsion to participate in the program. The scientist that doesn't care for any reason for seeking Monsanto support is under no obligation to do it. He simply seeks support elsewhere."

Monsanto includes other agreements in its strategy of covering each major area of technology development in biotechnology. They initiated a twelve-year, $23 million agreement with Harvard University. In addition they sponsor research at Oxford and Rockefeller Universities and belong to several university-based industrial liason programs. As part of their move into biotechnology they purchased G. D. Searle, the maker of aspartame and other biotech products. Finally, they have equity investments in Biogen, Genentech, and Genex, and they recently started a biotech company called Invitron. They are complementing these investments with a new $150 million life sciences center for in-house research.

Monsanto's Heinenger explains that the company has a strategy that won't fully pay off until the 1990's. Monsanto follows a set of principles in its dealings with universities: first, define needs and expectations of each partner at the outset; preserve academic freedom at all times; make the university understand the company's need for patent coverage; develop in-house skills to complement the university; a good communication system with the university must be in place; get ideas from multiple sources, seeking proposals from the younger scientists; encourage scientific peer review regularly, for both the projects and the overall relationship; be astute, being aware of when the research can pass on to the development stage. Heininger explains that rarely is there a product in mind when entering into these types of agreements; it is basic, directed research.

Other companies have made significant investments in basic research, thereby generating quite a bit of controversy. Hoechst AG made a surprising agreement with the Harvard-linked Massachusetts General Hospital, promising $70 million to build a new department of molecular biology where four Hoechst scientists could train with some of Harvard's best molecular biologists. Hoechst has exclusive rights to the work and must approve publication but it has no say on what work is to be conducted. This agreement sparked concern in Congress, where Congressman Albert Gore spearheaded a drive to investigate whether it is right for a foreign company to have such easy access to science which was developed by taxpayers' money. The fire has subsided, but Gore and other Congressmen continue to look carefully at the technology transfer taking place in biotechnology.

At Johnson & Johnson, a corporation which decentralizes its research and development activities, a corporate office was established in 1978 to help discover external scientific and technological resources applicable to the present or future business interests of its companies. Some of these fell between the interests at the individual companies. A further objective was to assist in exploiting these opportunities through the companies or by the establishment of programs outside the Corporation. By bringing in information from outside and by promoting increased communication between companies inside the corporation this office sought to help the companies upgrade their internal scientific competence. A "focused giving" program to provide support for basic research in the universities was established in 1980 and came under the administration of the Corporate Office of Science and Technology a year later. This program fits well with the objectives stated above and allowed the corporation to become involved in many university programs in biotechnology in addition to the research agreements individual companies had with outside interests. The corporation became further involved in outside research through its major research agreement with the Scripps Institute and set up a small research and development group in LaJolla to exploit the Scripps discoveries and transfer the technology to various Johnson & Johnson companies.

New technology from the outside was also acquired by the company through acquisition or equity investment in small entrepreneurial companies by the Johnson & Johnson Development Company.

Johnson & Johnson and other corporations donate money and resources to the universities as part of a good neighbor policy and to ensure that there is a new generation of talented researchers. Motorola and other semiconductor companies have formed the Semiconductor Research Corporation, a consortium of companies that support good contract research at a number of major universities. According to William Howard, Senior Vice President for corporate-directed R&D, Motorola is also involved in Stanford, Berkeley, and Texas. Because they wanted talented people to stay in their location, Phoenix, they participated in a rescue mission, getting companies to work together with government to bolster the resources of Arizona State University. Howard claims there are four reasons why Motorola has pursued a diversified program of supporting universities: it builds an impression upon candidates for jobs; it gives access to research results; it gets people at the student level aware of Motorola's products; and it promotes a good citizen image, especially in Arizona where Motorola is the largest employer in the state. In the case of Arizona State, they participated with Good Year Research and Honeywell in building a centers of excellence project. The university will be able to supply well-trained graduates for work at Motorola and Motorola can point to Arizona State as a place where a candidate for a position can train. It makes Phoenix a more attractive place for a researcher to move. Motorola is working on a similar program in Illinois. Called the Build Illinois program, it involves helping the Illinois Institute of Technology, Northwestern, and the University of Illinois at Chicago Circle.

A look at another major diversified corporation shows how involved companies can get with the university. Allied Corporation, whose products run from chemicals to aerospace and automotive products, gives unrestricted grant money to universities through its foundation. It also sponsors a great deal of contract research. It participates in industrial liason programs at MIT, Cal Tech, Rochester, University of Massachusetts, Rutgers and formerly at Purdue. It supports the Waxman Institute at Rutgers and has memberships in the Council for Chemical Research, The Chemical Industry Institute for Toxicology, and Microelectronics and Computer Technology Corporation (MCC). At the University of Rhode Island they are creating a special applied engineering laboratory, donating all equipment, and matching operating dollars that the university collects for the laboratory. Allied has over seventy-five research sites to accept technology transferred from the university.

At Cyanamid there's a big push on business development that extends over to the support of university projects, which are often less expensive than doing in-house research despite large overhead fees charged by universities. Besides direct support through grants, Cyanamid supports several research centers and recently helped Texas A&M University to set up its own research program. They're especially involved in a program at Columbia University, although they have contracts at the University of South Dakota and Penn State in mining, Yale and Delaware in catalysis, University of Massachusetts and New York Polytechnic Institute in polymers, and half a dozen key schools in organic synthesis. According to one Cyanamid executive, "I think the geography factor is a major one. Very, very major, in terms of interaction." He reported difficulty in getting staff members to go to a half-day meeting when travel makes it almost a three-day affair. He claims that top companies in the chemical industry shoot for 1 to 2 percent of their R&D budgets in university work. The situations of Hoechst and Monsanto are quite rare.

When business development requires it, the company can move a division to the site of the university, as Johnson & Johnson did with Salk and Kodak did with Cornell when it wanted to invest in biotechnology. In the case of Cornell, Kodak and several other major companies moved into an industrial park. Three major parks, Princeton's Forrestal Center, Stanford Industrial Park, and Research Triangle Park, attract businesses that want the prestige of being associated with the university and want close access to researchers. These corporations know that these select locations are also beneficial for recruiting from university laboratories, where researchers will want to be near their university colleagues and in a stimulating environment after making the transition from the university to industry. Companies pay premium rents in these locations.

In summary, it is evident that corporations are finding the university to be an increasingly attractive place to fund or conduct research; arriving at a time when grants are drying up, they are a welcome source of income for universities.

The threat to academic freedom by corporations has been debated, but the consensus is that the corporation does not want to change the role of the university. It simply wants to influence the university to do what it does best, but to do it in a direction that will benefit the company. There is little evidence that the university's basic research mission has been adversely affected. The corporations simply want to position themselves in a place where they can most easily and quickly commercialize the results. If the corporation's role as a grant-giver is compared with grant-giving government agencies like the National Science Foundation or the National Institutes of Health, it is evident that the corporation provides one additional option that, like the government grants, the research is free to explore or ignore. Yes, corporate grants will influence the direction of basic research because they are an attractive source of funds. Corporations are not interested in having basic researchers do applied work. They have their own staffs and agendas for doing applied work. They receive from the universities a basic understanding that will indirectly influence the amount of technology that the company can develop.

4   The Universities: Allies
with Industry

Universities are the strongholds of theoretical knowledge. Sometimes theoretical knowledge is necessary for technical progress to occur. At other times, industry can fashion its technology without the need for theory. As Motorola's E. David Metz points out, "It wasn't until this century that the crystal structure and hardening process of steel were understood on a theoretical basis. But you know that the Japanese have made very hard steel swords, steel outer coatings with a softer undercoating, for literally hundreds and hundreds of years."

In microelectronics, the theoretical basis for industry's technology was established in company laboratories. Only in the past few years has it been recognized that the university is in a position to play a major role in the technology's advancement if it is given the talent, time, and equipment to forge ahead. In biotechnology, by contrast, industrial innovation has been largely dependent upon the contributions of university scientists who have consulted for or migrated to industry. It has been said that it is virtually impossible to find a top microbiologist in an American university who does not have some industrial affiliation.

The role of the university in the commercialization process varies greatly from industry to industry. It is certain that biotechnology's dependence upon the university is unique. Technology transfer is rarely hoped for in university-industrial cooperative research enterprises. The university can offer, however, a theoretical knowledge base that has a long-term impact upon the direction of corporate research. More importantly, it can offer the talent of academic consultants and graduate students who will become tomorrow's industrial scientists.

A major study conducted by Lois Peters and Herbert Fusfeld of the Center for Science and Technology Policy for the National Science Board concluded that access to high quality manpower is the prime motivation underlying industry's desire to establish joint university-industry research programs.[1] The time-sensitivity and proprietary nature of corporate research tend to make support for product development efforts at universities nearly impossible for most companies.

Peters and Fusfeld conducted detailed surveys and site visits at ninety-six major universities, companies, and other institutions in order to understand more about the dynamics of corporate-university research relationships. They discovered that in the vast majority of cases the university initiated the interaction for cooperative research. Contrary to what one might expect, only in 15 percent of the cases did the company initiate the interaction. But industry is in general more concerned with staying close to potential personnel and getting a general overview of the science than with anything else. Biotechnology proves to be an exception to the pattern. Pharmaceutical, chemical and food-related companies have raced to universities to rapidly establish or expand their capabilities in applying molecular biology and bioengineering to their R&D programs. Much of this work has been conducted through specific research contracts.

Fusfeld explains:

When we asked the companies what is your reason for supporting research at universities or for having interaction with them, far and away the principal reason is access to people. How they get that access isn't critical, whether it's through scholarships or fellowships, through visits or through sponsoring research, but they do know they want certain types of people. Above everything else they want access to the trained specialized graduates in their fields.

Universities have become far more aggressive for corporate money in recent years. This has caused reorganization within the university to provide for a more activist role in obtaining money. Of the thirty-nine research universities visited by the Peters-Fusfeld study group, 50 percent had liason offices or positions and 50 percent of these were new positions or newly reorganized offices.

The main reason why universities cooperate with industry is to get a fresh supply of research money to help diversify the university's funding base. In the Peters-Fusfeld study, 41 percent of university administrators cited this as a prime motive for industrial cooperation. This is an especially important reason in an era of decreasing growth in federal support for university research. Another 36 percent of those interviewed supported corporate interactions because industrially sponsored research exposed students to real-world problems. Thirty-three percent of respondents favored corporate relations to provide better training for the increasing number of graduates going into industry, while 28 percent cited a preference for industrial money because it involved less red tape and fewer reporting requirements than government money.

One of the main concerns of university administrators is how the university can maintain its identity as a free disseminator of knowledge to society when it has so many relationships with the proprietary interests of companies. Most universities have insisted upon the right to publish results of industrially sponsored contract research with a minimal delay time for patent reviews by the sponsoring corporation. Universities have also taken steps to ensure that the interests of professors in working for companies do not interfere with their university research and teaching responsibilities.

Some of the ways in which basic knowledge is transferred from the university to the corporation include: placement of industrial scientists in university labs; visits to corporate sites by researchers or graduate students; consulting relationships with professors; use of industrial scientists as adjunct professors; placement of graduate students in industrial labs for internships; and continuing education programs.

The Council for Chemical Research asked its University-Industry Interaction Committee to survey chemistry department chairmen and their industrial counterparts about the value and amount of participation in university-industry cooperative programs. Those areas that rated highest in both value and participation include: faculty seminars on the industrial site; traditional consulting arrangements; individual visits to corporations by faculty to discuss research of mutual interest; invitations to attend university workshops; use of student interns at corporate sites for summer jobs; and sponsored research programs, including exchange of personnel. There are a variety of ways for universities to effectively disseminate new ideas to industry without compromising their freedom to communicate knowledge openly in the academic community. These means of transferring basic knowledge can be healthy for the university, exposing faculty and students to the industrial and ultimately the social benefits of their research. Exposure to large industry in these programs also works to the advantage of growing entrepreneurial firms like Genentech or Cetus that can promise an academic type of research atmosphere with the advantage of seeing the researcher's work bear fruit in society. These knowledge transfer vehicles are therefore vehicles for recruiting university talent for industry.

When actual technology, as opposed to basic knowledge, is transferred from the university to industry, it may involve the reorienting of basic researchers so that they become applied researchers in a corporate climate. Recruitment by industry of key graduate students in the lab of a professor who is involved in a cooperative research program might serve this objective. In a field like biotechnology, both the small entrepreneurial firms and the large chemical and pharmaceutical companies have been able to recruit some leading researchers away from the university. The university actively supports technology transfer when it offers facilities, professors' consulting time, rights to use university-developed technologies, or entrepreneurial programs that encourage new companies to form on or near campus. When the university allows a government extension service to operate on campus, it is encouraging technology transfer. When an institution like Ohio University builds an innovation center on campus to encourage professors to work for industry, it enhances technology transfer. If incubator facilities are located on campus to tap university talent for new, high technology ventures, technology transfer is served. Similarly, when a university like Stanford actively markets basic licenses to patents on genetic engineering techniques, it is aggressively transferring technology. Another form of technology transfer occurs when universities like Cornell, Rensselaer Polytechnic Institute or Stanford develop technology parks where growing companies can make use of nearby university facilities and university scientists for product development. When universities engage in government-industry-university consortium relationships to work on engineering problems, they are engaging in technology transfer.

Throughout these activities a common trend has emerged on the university's part toward greater interest in and cooperation with industry. Universities with strong research capabilities are, in some cases, changing their policies to allow cooperation to take place with minimal disruption of the university's traditional roles. Despite the trend toward cooperation, universities remain far more dependent upon federal government money than industrial money. Their patenting and licensing policies reflect this dependence and, in many cases, the research agreements arrived at with industry are modelled after the government grant-giving policies. Finally, it should be remembered that the trend toward university-industrial cooperation is having the most influence at only the largest and best-equipped, research-oriented institutions. Many colleges and small universities are immune to industry's advances because they have little to offer in terms of research talent or facilities. According to Fusfeld, American universities fall into three levels in terms of cooperation with industry.

There's the level of the majestic research university that literally wants its research to be as unfettered as possible and will accept money from industry only on the fairly severe condition that no special advantages are granted to the sponsor. There's the middle level group of universities that want very much to have industry money. They don't have the huge endowments of, for example, a Harvard. It must have its objectivity and independence, but it is perfectly willing to work out arrangements that will give some incentives to industries without limiting its ability to publish and choose its own direction of research. There's a third level of our institutions that don't do research. In fact, most institutions don't.

A close look at several of the major universities affected by these new trends sheds light on how the commercialization process of science is working.

CORNELL UNIVERSITY

Cornell University is an example of an institution that has committed itself to industrial alliances in many ways without sacrificing its basic research and teaching missions. It participates in federal and state technology development programs, a research consortium, an industrial park with an incubator program, and a multi-industrial research center.

A significant part of Cornell's commercialization activities centers around its resources in biotechnology. According to Ray Snyder, executive director of the Cornell biotechnology program, there are two components of the program. Cornell has established a Biotechnology

Institute with financial support from Eastman Kodak, General Foods and Union Carbide. Each company has committed itself to pay $2.5 million over a six-year period. In return, each gets to review research results before publication, has first refusal on licensing of any patents that stem from work they publish, and has royalty-free use of the material.

The other component of the biotechnology program results from Cornell's selection by New York State as a Center for Advanced Technology (CAT) in agricultural biotechnology. The CAT program provides $1 million and faculty-initiated research proposals are chosen by a board composed of Cornell faculty and representatives of each company. The CAT and the Institute fund the same types of projects but they never fund a project jointly. No distinction is made to identify a research project as CAT or institute-funded research. This policy gives Cornell researchers freedom to propose projects under a pool of funding of about $2.1 million a year, and it protects the rights of the corporations to all the research without regard to funding source.

According to Snyder, "the three partners that are with us—Kodak, General Foods and Union Carbide—are using the biotechnology program at Cornell to bring their biotechnology research up to snuff at whatever field they're interested in pursuing." Two of the industrial scientists are actually participating as part of the Cornell research team. In addition, they have access to all university facilities, "like a visiting academic person on campus."

Any faculty member on campus is eligible to apply for a grant through the program. Some of the current research efforts include: genetic engineering of chloroplasts in plants; the genetics and biochemistry of microorganisms in dairy fermentation; and the introduction of new genetic material into chicken embryos.

Cornell established its industry research park near the campus back in 1967. It has operated as a type of incubator facility for the past four years. The park currently contains twenty-one corporate tenants, fourteen of which are high-technology companies. There are three types of tenants, according to Tom Mailey, director of the facility: companies based on technologies developed by Cornell staff or faculty; companies that are located near Cornell to access Cornell consulting talent, equipment or other resources; and local people who have developed new technologies. Cornell's basic role is to act as landlord for all these tenants and facilitate shared service usage.

The program has plenty of room for new companies to expand. According to Mailey, "It's part of our plan for companies to move from the incubator facility into a multitenant facility right at the research park as their second home and eventually go into their third home while still being a tenant at research park." So far, no companies have graduated from the incubator. The oldest company is five years old, and most companies are less than four years old.

Mailey claims that the incubator concept originated many years ago in Europe but only became popular in the United States in recent years. Previously, venture capitalists used their own facilities as incubators, keeping watch over management and supplying secretarial and other services as needed. The concept of the incubator is to provide services to new companies in a cost-effective way while offering consulting and advice tailored to the needs of young firms. The startup company needs a range of support services that it doesn't use on a full-time basis. For instance, there are certain administrative, clerical and secretarial services that a company can't justify on a full-time basis when it's first starting. It needs conference rooms and seminars, and it needs to be in with other companies and other groups that are essentially in the same state. Mailey finds it helpful for tenants to identify and resolve problems that they have in common. In many cases this leads to collaboration, including the sharing of staff and resources and the bartering of consulting talents.

Working together in the incubator can have other advantages as well. Suppliers will visit a facility with a group of small companies, but they would not be likely to seek out companies of this size if they were spread out across the region. Mailey also finds that venture capitalists will come to the incubator when they realize they can visit several companies in one day. The research park director can serve as a promoter for these sources of badly needed money.

Cornell has several programs in the microelectronics area that involve industrial participation. The university has been selected as a center of excellence by the Semiconductor Research Association (SRC), a consortium of companies that funds advanced research work at universities. Nowell MacDonald, the director of the program at Cornell, explains that rapid transfer of technology is one objective of this program. "I think the companies that send people here since they want to pick up research do the best in technology transfer." MacDonald explains that SRC has topical conferences and what he calls "technology transfer presentations'' that are very good for informing industries on a monthly basis about what is taking place at the university. The SRC program at Cornell draws upon about twenty-four professors and thirty-five graduate students in the materials science, electrical engineering, applied physics, and physics departments. The program is examining the next two generations of microelectronic circuits with an annual budget of $1.7 million.

Cornell sponsors a unique program for corporations that want to look at the industrial potential of structures that are smaller than one micron. The program, PROSUS, or the Cornell Program on Submicrometer Structures, is affiliated with the campus-based National Research and Resource Facility for Submicron Structures. The facility has been constructed and maintained with National Science Foundation support since 1977. The goal of the program is to understand how to make very small structures and what happens in them once they are made. One obvious application of this work is in the semiconductor industry for building supersmall and superfast conductors. The program's projects also include studies of metals, electron flow, ions, X rays, lasers, optical phenomena, and construction of devices that measure these entities at the smallest level. For $15,000 per year companies can join PROSUS and stay informed through the leading academic programs in the United States on submicrometer structures. There are currently thirty-five corporate members. Their contributions support the work of 40 faculty members and nearly 200 affiliated faculty, staff, and students conducting about 106 active research projects. The Cornell faculty reviews this research for corporate members at periodic meetings on campus. In addition, faculty members visit company locations or invite company staff to visit them at Cornell. The PROSUS program also includes updating of members through technical newsletters and other distributions of information. Finally, PROSUS provides opportunities for joining industrial-academic research on campus.

Current cooperative efforts in the national submicron facility include about eight industrial companies and eighteen universities. The facility is run with about $1.6 million from the NSF and about $500,000 from industry. According to its director, Edward Wolf, there are 120 graduate students working on about 100 research projects in 9 different disciplines, primarily in electrical engineering, materials science and applied physics. The policy board governing the program is a mix of academic and industrial scientists.

RENSSELAER POLYTECHNIC INSTITUTE

Rensselaer Polytechnic Institute (RPI) has taken a leadership role in industry-university interactions, promoting three industrial innovation centers, an incubator facility, a technology park, and a major facility in the planning stage to link the innovation centers.

The Center for Interactive Computer Graphics was established on campus in 1979 with $270,000 in support from the National Science Foundation through its University-Industry Cooperative Research Program. Under the terms of the NSF agreement, the Center had to become self-supporting through industrial funding within three years. The program has been a spectacular success. It now has about forty-five companies paying $40,000 per year to join, according to RPI's Chris LeMaistre, director of the Center for Industrial Innovation. The Industrial Associates help provide guidelines for the research in the program. The companies now share in about $1.6 million worth of research. They receive semiannual reviews on the projects, they can pursue their own sponsored research with the center, and they have the opportunity to recruit students. The program is especially helpful to graduate students, who often get summer jobs with sponsoring companies. Major sponsors include IBM, General Electric, Kodak, Union Carbide, Sikorsky, and Data General.

In May of 1979 RPI launched a second center, the Center for Manufacturing Productivity and Technology Transfer. Initial seed money of $1.1 million came from the General Electric Company, Boeing, and General Motors. There are now about twelve founding companies, including IBM, Digital Equipment Corporation, Alcoa and United Technologies. These companies each pay $300,000 to join the Center. "The intent of the Center," according to LeMaistre, "was to project manufacturing as being a good career opportunity for bright young engineers." Sponsoring companies also conduct contract research in the Center. The program is unique in having paid project managers instead of faculty members to oversee the work of the graduate and undergraduate students. Faculty members interact as advisers to graduate students and as consultants to the project managers. One area investigated at the Center is how integrated circuits can be used in novel ways in the manufacturing process.

The third industrial center at RPI is the Center for Integrated Electronics (CIE). Work at the CIE focuses on the development of highly sophisticated, very large scale integrated (VLSI) circuits. RPI benefits from the use of an advanced electron beam lithography system, a direct-write EL-2 donated by IBM. The EL-2 uses electronic beams to etch the fine connector lines that link electronic components on a chip and allow electrical current to pass through them. About $12 million worth of equipment has been donated by industry to the Center.

The CIE was founded with the support of Computervision Corporation, Digital Equipment Corporation, General Electric, and IBM. Other sponsoring companies include Fairchild Semiconductor, Harris Semiconductor, Sperry and Xerox, with a total of seventeen leading supporters. The Center benefits from industrial membership on its Technical Visiting Committee which advises on CIE's technical direction and a Founders Committee which advises on broad policy issues and the Center's overall operations.

The CIE raised about $30 million for advanced research. The Center's enrollment is 250, with 100 graduate students, a full-time staff of 15, and 25 participating faculty. Research funding should be about $3 million per year.

The success of these three centers plus other industrial initiatives led the then president of RPI, George Low, to lobby with New York State's then governor Hugh Carey for additional funding for university programs. When he met with Governor Carey, Low brought along the chief executive officers of five of the leading New York State corporations. Low argued that since New York's smokestack industries were dying, there was a desperate need in the state for a focal point and a catalyst for high technology. Low suggested that RPI, with its excellent track record, could play a major role in this effort. Carey agreed and an interest-free loan of $30 million was arranged to build a Center for Industrial Innovation (CII) on campus. The Center for Interactive Graphics, the Center for Manufacturing Productivity and the Center for Electronics are housed in the CII. RPI plans to invest an additional $30 million of its own money into hardware and equipment for the facility. The CII will act as a liason with industry, providing continuing education through an interactive television system. It expects to sponsor a complete spectrum of accredited graduate courses.

RPI also has a very successful incubator program. According to Jerry Mahoney, a banker and the director, the program is unique in specializing in high-technology companies. About fifteen companies currently use the facility, which includes secretarial and answering services, and a personnel service to help locate employees, students, and faculty members who can assist new businesses. Mahoney screens the potential occupants closely, checking business plans before space is allocated. He acts as a business and financial resource, directing venture capitalists to companies when appropriate. Occupants of the incubator benefit from hard wiring to the campus computer, and they have the use of the various facilities on campus.

The university also started to develop and market a technology park in 1982. RPI has set aside 1,200 acres of their own land near campus for this purpose. National Semiconductor was the first tenant, moving its optoelectronics division there from California's Silicon Valley. Another tenant, PacAmOr Bearings—a company that markets precision miniature ball bearings—has built its own building. There are about fifteen businesses and more than 300 employees in the park.

MASSACHUSETTS INSTITUTE OF TECHNOLOGY

The Massachusetts Institute of Technology (MIT) has a long heritage of cooperation with industry. This cooperation was clearly articulated in the institute's charter in 1861, which stated one of MIT's goals as "instituting and maintaining . . . a school of industrial science and aiding generally by suitable means, the advancement, development, and practical application of science in connection with the arts, agriculture, manufactures and commerce." With an annual research budget of nearly $400 million, it is a leader in knowledge and technology transfer as well as an important source of talent for high-technology innovation. According to James Utterback, director of the MIT Industrial Liaison Program, it is estimated that faculty, staff, and students from MIT have started over 1,000 technology-based companies in the Boston area alone.

One of the greatest resources for industry is the MIT Industrial Liaison Program, which boasts a membership of 300 companies on four continents. Founded in 1948, it provides a network for quickly and efficiently communicating the breadth of the university's research to participating corporations. Members are given an annual directory summarizing more than 3,000 research projects at the university. When they join, member companies are assigned to one of seventeen liason officers, scientists with advanced degrees and industrial experience who will guide members through the MIT research maze and arrange for meetings with faculty members on campus or at the industrial site. A staff of forty provides essential services to the program, including a newsletter, technical publications, and an invaluable series of fifteen to twenty symposia held each year at MIT and various locations. Short courses and seminars are also held in Japan and Europe for the benefit of foreign member companies. These symposia inform members of the latest developments in key areas of science and technology at MIT.

In addition to the Industrial Liaison Program, MIT sponsors about a dozen industrial collegia. The collegium is a format that enables a group of companies with interests in a particular field to fund the relevant research at MIT. Special publications, seminars, workshops and personnel exchanges are used as vehicles to communicate the results of the research. Program companies get royalty-free, non-exclusive licenses and receive a share of any royalty income earned by MIT from licenses to non-members. The institute started its first collegium, the Polymer Processing Program, in 1973 with funding from the NSF. Today it is supported entirely by twelve founding companies. Other programs currently exist in communications, construction, physics, manufacturing technology, chemistry, materials and economics. Members of the Industrial Liaison Program are given special discounts as enticements to join the collegium program.

MIT acts as a knowledge-transfer agent to industry through its extensive sponsored research program. Companies usually get nonexclusive, royalty-free licenses to exploit results of research that they fund individually at the university. The largest contract so far is an agreement formed in 1980 with Exxon Research and Engineering Company. Exxon is providing $8 million over ten years for basic research in combustion science. Eight to twelve projects are funded at any given time under the direction of a committee of four Exxon researchers and four MIT faculty members.

In 1982 MIT formed another agreement, this time with W.R. Grace. This supports the departments of chemistry, chemical engineering and biology to conduct experiments on the production of amino acids and enzymes by fermentation and chemical methods of separation and pu-

rification. W.R. Grace is financing the program for five years at $6 to
$8.5 million. Some projects may entail giving exclusive licenses to
Grace, but others involve non-exclusive, royalty-free licenses. MIT
can license these patents to other companies for a fee. About 20 percent of the company's funding will provide general support for MIT
research without any commitment to Grace.

Technology licensing from MIT is a significant source of technology transfer to industry. A close look at MIT's licensing policy shows
how industrially oriented the university is. MIT policy allows each
sponsored research agreement to be negotiated individually. Normally
the university owns the patent and licenses it to the sponsor. Under
exceptional circumstances MIT is allowed to grant patent ownership
to the sponsor. MIT breaks down the royalties it receives so that the
inventor and the department each get a share. Usually the inventor gets
35 to 15 percent, the amount decreasing with the size of the royalty.
The department gets 5 to 25 percent of the share, the amount increasing with the size of the royalty. In any case, MIT only keeps 60 percent of its rightful royalties and distributes the rest.

MIT stipulates in its policy that if an invention makes significant
use of funds, space or facilities but there is no contractual obligation
to another party, the invention becomes the property of MIT. There is
one exception to this rule: if a student is the inventor, MIT will waive
its rights. In this case, 60 percent of royalties go to MIT, 35 to 15
percent goes to the inventor, and the department gets 5 to 25 percent.
As another part of its policy, MIT allows the inventor to own all rights
to the invention when there has been no significant use of funds, space
or MIT facilities.

YALE UNIVERSITY

Yale University conducts a great deal of basic research, but this is
largely funded by the federal government. The university has taken
several steps over the past few years to cooperate more with industry.
The result has been an increase in private support for the university,
changes in faculty policies, and the development of an industrial research park.

Yale currently holds two large sponsored research contracts. The
first is a three-year contract initiated in 1982 with the Celanese Corporation. Celanese is contributing $1.1 million to fund research on

enzymes, a new product area for the company. The agreement pays for postdoctoral students and technicians in the laboratories of L. Nicholas Ornston. Celanese retains the exclusive license to all of the work it funds.

The second agreement provides for Bristol-Myers to support the Department of Pharmacology with $3 million over five years. The department is conducting general research on anti-cancer drugs, which Bristol-Myers is screening for potential effectiveness. Bristol-Myers gets an exclusive license to all work produced on anti-cancer drugs by scientists named in the agreement. In addition, the company has the right of first refusal to licenses on other projects by the same faculty.

In response to the increasing number of interactions between industry and the university, Yale revised its policies to be sure that academic goals are not compromised while the university enjoys the maximum benefits of industrial support. In March of 1984 the Committee on Cooperative Research, Patents and Licensing issued its final report, finding it necessary to add to the Faculty Handbook a sentence stating that Yale shall not enter into any agreement that prohibits free and open discussion of ongoing research. The new policy does not allow research agreements where Yale faculty are not permitted to withdraw from sponsored research programs; in addition, Yale will not allow constraint on the activities of those who withdraw from sponsored programs.

The new policy reaffirms that faculty can consult for no more than one day per week, but it specifies that under no circumstances should communication of results of university research be suppressed. Faculty members must disclose the nature and extent of professional and consulting activities. In addition, faculty members have to inform the president or provost of any management or significant ownership in an enterprise that makes commercial use of his or her academic or professional endeavors. These activities are reviewed by a committee designated by the provost to ensure that they fall within university policies.

The university, like many others in recent years, has expanded its capacities to license and market technologies to industry. Yale, which previously used Research Corporation to handle its patents, now conducts all its own affairs through its recently formed Office of Cooperative Research. Under a new policy, the inventor gets 30 percent of net royalty income up to $200,000 and 20 percent of net for anything in excess of that amount. Another 30 percent of the net goes to the department. In order to encourage collaboration, when all principal investigators agree in advance to share in royalty income, the university will commit an additional 50 percent of its own royalty income to that department or facility.

Yale's criteria for licensing patents is similar in some respects to MIT's. It seeks "the most effective means of ensuring that the public reap the potential benefits of its research." This means that although non-exclusive licenses are ordinarily granted for sponsored research, exclusive licenses should be allowed if the cost and risk of the project would otherwise deter commercialization.

In keeping with Yale's new openness to industrial involvement, it has participated in the construction of New Haven Science Park, an incubator and large industrial facility that will allow some of the technology developed at Yale to diffuse into the industrial community. The project was started by the mayor of New Haven, the president of Yale, and the president of the Olin Corporation with financial assistance from the state of Connecticut. The park was conceived as an urban renewal project as well as an effort to stimulate industrial innovation. Olin and Yale donated space and a building near the Yale campus to start the park. The eighty-acre facility has resulted so far in fifty-two entrepreneurial, startup and support companies. It has led to the creation of 413 new jobs in the incubator within eighteen months. IBM is supporting a business training program in the park. In addition, there is a job corps program for youths of eighteen to twenty-four years that will train them for jobs in the park.

Science Park has established a New Enterprise Center on the premises to offer assistance in administrative services, business management, and access to capital. In the future, Science Park hopes to recruit some large, established companies. Its goal is to support 150 companies in the park.

According to Science Park's director, Henry Chauncey, the facility was modelled in some ways after Philadelphia's University City Science Center, another center where urban renewal was a focus. Science Park is in a state enterprise zone and expects to be in a federal enterprise zone. This means that rent and property taxes are relatively low and business taxes for equipment are abated for a number of years. There are additional measures for tax relief because of the park's status. Finally, employers in Science Park get job credits from the state in the form of cash advances for hiring people.

Science Park has taken some important additional steps to encourage entrepreneurs. For example, there are no leases in the park unless a business wants one. This is a nonthreatening policy for the entrepreneur who is unsure of his cash commitments. Science Park has also arranged for first-class professional services at reduced rates for its occupants. For example, lawyers and accountants give their first three hours for free. They allow clients to pay only half their fees for additional hours for the first three years of business.

Yale decided to participate in Science Park for several reasons. The park offers badly needed jobs for students and spouses in a city where unemployment is very high. Secondly, according to Chauncey there was a growing question in the Yale community about how the business community could properly interact with the university. It was decided that the best structure was to have an independent entity in which certain types of joint and cooperative research could take place rather than have it take place directly in the institution. Located adjacent to the Yale campus, Science Park is a convenient place for university spin-offs to set up shop. Another advantage of the park is that it allows the wealthy university to make a worthwhile contribution to the depressed New Haven area. Yale considers help to the community to be a major responsibility. If they are successful in developing this park, it will be the largest taxpayer in the city.

The Olin Corporation has much to gain from the park, which includes some building space donated by the corporation. Olin recently moved a major part of its company out of New Haven, causing additional unemployment. With three divisions of the corporation remaining in the city, Olin is anxious to maintain its environment and its image in the community. Building the park offers Olin important tax advantages as well as good public relations.

STANFORD UNIVERSITY

Stanford University is a rich source of knowledge for industrial innovation. A number of enterprising companies in biotechnology and microelectronics, for example, have spun off from research conducted there. Major patents, including the fundamental Cohen-Boyer patent for gene splicing, have led to standard industrial techniques in a number of fields.

The most interesting example of cooperative research at Stanford is the Center for Integrated Systems (CIS). It was founded as a response to the need to integrate several subdisciplines to investigate concepts and design VLSI systems for computers. It was also created to educate a new type of technical leader capable of conducting integrated research. CIS was founded in 1980. Its first industrial support came from pledges of $750,000 each for three years by General Electric, Hewlett Packard, TRW, Northrop, Xerox, Texas Instruments, Fairchild, Honeywell, IBM and Tektronix. Companies that later joined include Digital Equipment Corporation, Intel, ITT, GTE, Motorola, United Technologies, Monsanto, Gould/AMI, Philips Signetics and Rockwell. They have collectively contributed $15 million for the design and construction of a 70,000 square-foot building to house the Center. Eighty manufacturers of fabrication equipment have contributed equipment worth $6 million. In addition to initial industrial efforts, CIS received incremental funding of $8 million from the Department of Defense to support its launch.

Autonomous project teams led by Stanford faculty members carry out the CIS programs. Some research projects include: knowledge-based VLSI systems (the application of artificial intelligence); VLSI information systems; VLSI computer systems; medical and rehabilitative electronic sensors, circuits and systems; a computer-aided, fast-turnaround lab for wafer fabrication and testing; integrated-circuit process models; compound semiconductors and silicon-on-insulator research; and fundamental studies of semiconductor surfaces and interfaces. Each company participating in the program is allowed to send resident scientists to work with the Stanford teams.

As far as return on the $750,000 investment is concerned, director John Linville says,

This was made as a contribution so there really isn't a quid pro quo. It was Stanford's intent at the beginning that CIS sponsors have facilitated access to our graduate students and to our research. What do I mean by facilitated access? The university is open and consequently anyone can come and get information, but for sponsors we organize that information.

CIS will train one hundred master's level students and thirty Ph.D.s per year, good candidates for industry. In addition, VLSI research conducted at CIS should help give participating companies a competitive advantage in designing and fabricating their own chips.

HARVARD UNIVERSITY

Harvard is no stranger to cooperative research with industry. It signed an agreement in 1974 with the Monsanto Company that provides $23 million to the university over twelve years. The research grant supports the study of the biology and biochemistry of organ development. One result of the project is a bone-growth inducer that Monsanto is commercializing.

Harvard President Derek Bok debated a proposal in 1980 for Harvard to become a minority shareholder in a new biotechnology venture to be formed around the work of one of its scientists, Mark Ptashne. According to the proposal, Harvard would retain 10 to 15 percent of the stock as well as royalty income from patents. The issue was fully debated at a meeting of the faculty of the Arts and Sciences as well as the Council of Deans and the elected Council for the Faculty of Arts and Sciences. The debate unearthed widespread concern that there were too many conflicts of interest for the university to be so closely involved in a major concern. Harvard has to judge use of laboratory space, leaves of absence for professors, training of graduate students, and other areas where the financial interest might compete with the pure academic interest. By facing the issue squarely and debating it openly, Harvard set some limits on commercialization that other universities have studied and modelled.

A more traditional cooperative research agreement was signed in 1981 for DuPont to provide Harvard with $6 million for genetics research under the direction of Philip Leder. According to the agreement, there are no restrictions for research publication or communication with colleagues. Harvard retains all patents but DuPont gets exclusive licenses to all patentable research. The point of the research, however, it not so much the products that immediately result but the access to research intelligence that can be used to strengthen DuPont's in-house research efforts. Leder has been working on the mechanisms by which genes assemble the globin protein in hemoglobin and assemble antibodies.

As we shall see in Chapter 9, the advance of industry to campus brings with it a host of risks and potential conflicts of interest. The basic issues include the university's ability to maintain an atmosphere of open communication; the creation of researchers who might place great emphasis on applied research at the expense of basic research;

and the possible transfer of U.S. basic scientific expertise to international competitors through foreign funding of universities. These issues can be resolved by universities, as Yale has attempted to do, but they require careful monitoring by industry, the academic institutions, and individual scientists to maintain the proper balance between institutions.

The universities cited are examples of the trend toward greater participation by industry in the university's research life. It will yield a new generation of university-trained scientists who have familiarity with industry. This will make industry more attractive to the scientist, ultimately broadening and improving the research base for American companies.

5 Federal and State Assistance for High Technology

High technology has earned a starring role in the efforts by state governments to revitalize their economies and build an infrastructure for their future financial health. According to a 1983 report from the U.S. Congressional Office of Technology Assessment, programs are under way in at least thirty-eight states to attract new ventures and large corporations to spend their high technology dollars there.[1] The payoff for the region includes increases in corporate tax revenues and employment, upgrading of the educational systems, and development of service industries to high-technology-based businesses. The federal government also has programs to directly and indirectly encourage the development of high technology.

Participating states and regions devise their own formulas for assistance. However, a survey of the field reveals that there are a limited number of tactics available. Each player chooses an enticement based on existing strengths and an analysis of how to attract new business. Standard lures include: tax forgiveness; offers to assist in obtaining new venture capital money; incubator space where young companies can start up inexpensively; matching funding; employee training; help with financing for buildings or research and development; and offers to coordinate local resources, including services that help firms find talent and additional money.

Entrepreneurially minded administrators are finding new methods to apply established state and federal programs to encourage technological innovation. There is also a movement in state and federal governments to develop ingenious new programs that benefit the economy by supporting high technology development.

FEDERAL GOVERNMENT PROGRAMS

The federal government is providing assistance through tax-related legislation, economic development bonds, loans and grants, and new programs that stress collaboration between government, universities, and industry.

The National Science Foundation (NSF) has played a major role in the effort to encourage collaboration. Its newest program in this area includes establishment of various Engineering Research Centers located at universities throughout the United States. During the first year of operation in 1985, the NSF started six of these centers, with plans for more centers in future years. According to Eric Bloch, Director of the NSF, "the basic idea behind this new program is to help university researchers develop long-term, fundamental knowledge on engineering problems of significance to industry and to educate a new generation of students who can readily integrate ideas and techniques from a wide range of scientific and engineering disciplines." The purpose is to enhance industrial competitiveness internationally for U.S. products and to supply American industry with a steady stream of well-trained graduates.

The first six centers are backed by $94.5 million over a period of five years. They include a robotics systems in microelectronics center at the University of California, Santa Barbara ($14 million); a telecommunications program at Columbia University ($20 million); composites manufacturing at the University of Delaware in Newark in collaboration with Rutgers University ($7.5 million); systems research at the University of Maryland, College Park, in collaboration with Harvard University ($16 million); biotechnology process engineering at MIT ($20 million); and intelligent manufacturing systems at Purdue University ($17 million). After initial peer review, proposals were judged by a panel of engineers and scientists, four from academia and ten from industry. Bloch claims that "the new centers will promote strong links among universities, industry, and state governments."

The Engineering Research Centers program joins two older collaborative programs at NSF. The Industry/University Cooperative Research Projects Program was initiated to encourage direct collaboration between industrial and university scientists on selected projects. Research in the program does not focus on product development but on fundamental scientific and engineering questions. The projects must prove, however, to be relevant to future technologies or industrial use. Proposals are submitted jointly by the company and the university; the company must show seriousness of intent by sharing a significant part of its research costs. Another related program, the Industry/University Cooperative Research Centers Program, develops university-based centers on topics of interest to industry and universities with the provision that industry take on full support of the project within five years. These projects are too large to be supported by one company. The university must garner industrial support for the early phases of the project with the provision that this funding must increase until industrial support is complete.

These three programs show that the National Science Foundation is reaching far beyond its established role as an educational and research agency. It encourages innovation, directly concerning itself with how science can be applied by industry. In another new project, NSF will run the National Advanced Scientific Computing Centers with joint funding by universities and industry. Four centers have been named at four locations: the University of California at San Diego, the University of Illinois at Urbana-Champaign, Cornell University, and the John von Neumann Center near Princeton. As part of the collaboration, corporations will be donating "supercomputer" equipment—high-speed, high-load equipment that will train the next generation of computer scientists for industry. The Cray Corporation will provide its XMP computer to the University of California, San Diego, with connection to eighteen other universities. Cray will also supply equipment to Cornell; IBM's investment in the center tops $30 million. Exxon, American Telephone & Telegraph, and the Lockheed Corporation are assisting the Princeton center. The results of much of the research conducted with the new equipment should help industry. For example, the University of Illinois plans studies on the redesign of chemical processing plants and faster semiconductors, and it may involve itself in designs for aircraft and autos.

The NSF also spearheaded a program that eventually grew to include twelve research funding agencies in the federal government. In 1977 it started the Small Business Innovation Research program (SBIR) to help government, small high-technology firms, larger industrial firms, universities, and venture capital groups work together. The goal is to support small businesses that have innovative product ideas. During Phase I of the program, eligible small businesses may be awarded up to $50,000 for approximately six months to test the feasibility of the research idea in question. If the company passes this test, it may be eligible for Phase II funding of up to $500,000, usually for two years. Under Phase III of the project, the company must seek a venture capitalist, a large corporation, or some other private backer to continue research and development. Private investment now exceeds $60 million for the NSF program. For those who passed through the first two phases, private investment has been eight times the government support, and employment in these companies has increased by 125 percent. University involvement in these programs seems to be high. In 1983, 52 out of 102 Phase I NSF contracts were coupled to universities.

The NSF program has been so successful that it was copied under the Small Business Innovation Development Act of 1982. The Act stipulates that twelve federal agencies, each with R&D budgets in excess of $100 million, set aside 1.25 percent of their main research budget to fund small businesses. Two thousand awards for a total of $1.2 billion will be spent in the program by mid-1988.

The U.S. Department of Commerce is helping cooperative research through its Office of Productivity, Technology, and Innovation (OPTI). In order for American industry to better compete with industrial consortia established in Japan and Europe, Assistant Secretary D. Bruce Merrifield has started the Industrial Technology Partnership program (ITP). The ITP assists the private sector in making maximum use of cooperative or joint R&D ventures and R&D limited partnerships. As we shall examine further in Chapter 10, the R&D limited partnership is a mechanism that allows companies to fund research without taking the risk of investment upon themselves. Investors called limited partners bear the risk by funding the research, and receive significant tax benefits in return. The ITP promotes R&D limited partnerships, some of which fund university research on a contract basis. It offers workshops, a clearinghouse of specialized information on limited partnerships, special assistance to small businesses, introductory training on setting up partnerships, and a database of technical and marketing data that may be useful in drafting business plans.

The federal government has enacted several laws that aid high-tech industries. For example, President Reagan signed the National Cooperative Research Act of 1984, a law that provides that the courts cannot make joint research ventures unlawful per se simply because participating companies have large market shares. Until that time, antitrust guidelines stated that only companies with less than a 25 percent market share could participate in new joint ventures. High technology got a boost three years previously with the Economic Recovery Tax Act of 1981. This bill made capital investment in plants more cost-effective, speeding development of technology. The act supplied a 25 percent incremental tax credit for increased R&D expenditures and made equipment donations to universities more attractive.

Although tax and antitrust legislation can improve the climate for entrepreneurial science, the government can do a great deal to transfer some of its stockpile of federally funded technology directly to industry, resulting in increased product development.

State and local governments are taking advantage of other federal programs that have important if indirect effects upon regional high technology development. Community Development block grants have been used creatively in local regions for high tech. Innovators have developed incubators and industrial parks with the assistance of Urban Development Action Grants (UDAG) and local industry. New Haven Science Park, created by Yale University and the Olin Corporation, used UDAG funds for site preparation. Biomedical Research Park in Chicago has also benefited from UDAG grants. The city and state worked there to help Applied Molecular Genetics secure a $2 million UDAG. University City Science Center in Philadelphia used a $5 million UDAG to construct a residential and conference center. Another UDAG grant of $1.3 million was used to purchase a building for the Business and Technology Center in Philadelphia, a high technology center in a surrounding industrial park. These funds, when used creatively, can be very beneficial in developing high technology centers.

Another important source of federal funding for high technology are Industrial Revenue Bonds (IRBs). According to the OTA, "IRBs dwarf all other forms of state and local development resources, and they represent a crucial element in many high technology development initiatives." IRBs totalled $20 billion in 1981. New Haven's Science Park depended upon IRBs, which are exempt from all federal taxes.

The federal government also supplies funding through grants and loans from the Economic Development Administration. High technology agencies that have taken advantage of their planning and revolving loan funds include the Massachusetts Technology Development Corporation ($3 million); the Connecticut Product Development Corporation ($1 million); and the New York Science and Technology Foundation ($1 million).

STATE GOVERNMENT PROGRAMS

The OTA report, *Technology, Innovation and Regional Economic Development*, examined the strategies of state initiatives in a detailed survey.[2] It concluded, "state officials consider their high technology initiatives to be a natural and even inevitable extension of their different economic development strategies." States with better developed infrastructures in high technology, such as California and Massachusetts, are able to draw upon their established institutions for economic development, including venture capital development funds, regional development assistance offices, and ongoing university-industry technology transfer programs. Success in regional development for high technology often depends upon making traditional state programs work in innovative ways and coupling these programs with complementary programs such as job training or improvement of education.

High technology innovation at the state level can spring from a variety of sources. In the OTA survey of sixteen states, the governor's office was the instigator in more than half of the programs. State legislatures play a varying role; some make little or no effort, while others lead the initiatives in the state.

Many states seem to be competing for high-technology firms to settle in their regions. The surge in high technology state programs within the last five years might give the impression that states are relying upon entrepreneurial science for a quick fix for their economies. It is well known to these developers, however, that the number of new jobs directly created by entrepreneurial firms is relatively small. In certain fields such as biotechnology, innovation is dependent upon a modest number of Ph.D.s. States are looking instead to the indirect benefits of high technology development. A Task Force on Technological Innovation of the National Governor's Association confirms this conclusion. It reports that short-term efforts by most states to compete for technology-based research and manufacturing firms are accompanied by medium- and long-term strategies to encourage modernization in traditional industries. State governments expect a diffusion of technology to take place, creating innovation in the older smokestack industries through the existence of newer, high-tech firms. There are signs that this diffusion is already taking place, for example, in the chemical industry through biotechnology. The Task Force also reports that these long-term strategies include using high-technology firms to help create an environment that fosters entrepreneurial activity. Although incentives from state to state may appear similar, states use high-technology firms to produce innovation in ways that are distinctive to each region. Within a national economy that rewards entrepreneurship, the revitalization of industry at the state level works to help the national economy grow. The modernization of the economy in each state encourages economies of other states dependent upon that region to modernize. The development of telecommunications software in Silicon Valley, for example, revitalizes commerce in New York that extensively uses telecommunications for the banking and entertainment industries.

The reduction of federal economic aid programs has forced state governments to play larger roles in developing their high tech economies. The states have in many cases turned to the expertise of the private sector for its experience in high technology development. They have also tapped private industry's ability to foster innovation through contributions and donations of technical equipment to local and state universities. State governments have encouraged industry to provide risk capital, make site location decisions affecting high technology development, offer entrepreneurship training and assistance, and act as an advocate to get other firms to support high technology innovation. In return, the state can offer to established industry access to the tools it needs to modernize its manufacturing. For example, the government of Pennsylvania uses the Pennsylvania Technical Assistance program to supply technical information and assistance for technology transfer to all businesses in the state. The state government can also help to retrain workers in businesses that modernize their production technologies. A study by the OTA found that about half of all state high technology initiatives involved high technology training or education programs. The state government can also supply industry with managers who are trained in entrepreneurial skills. In 1983 the OTA identified fifteen state government initiatives undertaken with state universities to train entrepreneurs and inventors with the skills necessary to commercialize products.

A close look at several state programs will demonstrate some of the creativity used by state governments to make high technology development a reality.

New Jersey

New Jersey has the largest and most ambitious new program for industrial innovation in the nation. Passage of a $90 million high technology bond issue in 1984 has provided enough funding to carry out extensive revitalization plans recommended by a blue-ribbon governor's commission. The program emphasizes building up the educational and research base of the state to train the scientists of the future, renew the established pharmaceutical and chemical companies in the state with cooperative academic-industrial research, and create a climate attractive to entrepreneurial high-technology firms. The bond allots $57 million for advanced technology centers, $23 million for undergraduate technical and engineering facilities, $7 million for developing robotics and engineering training facilities, and $3 million for future needs.

The advanced technology centers, located at the state's major universities and medical schools, are centers where industry and academia will jointly fund and accomplish advanced applied research. Various private industry affiliates programs will be formed with paid memberships, matching grants and other forms of support. Four centers will be created in biotechnology ($20 million), hazardous and toxic substance management ($7 million), industrial ceramics ($9 million) and food technology ($6 million).

The heart of the biotechnology center will be a $23.6 million core facility to be built on the adjoining campuses of Rutgers University and the University of Medicine and Dentistry of New Jersey (UMDNJ). Both schools will jointly match the $20 million funding by the state to create a center with both an educational and a research focus that will be shared by industry and academia. The center will also be an instrumentation resource that will be made available to both industrial and academic researchers. In addition to the core facility, there will be a new fermentation pilot plant at the Waksman Institute of Rutgers and a clinical research center at Middlesex General-University Hospital.

According to Lawrence Edelman, interim director of the program, small industry will benefit enormously from collaborative research opportunities. Small industry will find this is a place where they can get things done that they simply couldn't get any other way. This will be a magnet to the small hi-biotech kinds of industry that tend to grow up around universities that have intensive efforts in that field.

The program provides for the advancement of molecular genetics, molecular cell biology, and molecular and cellular pharmacology in the state. The plan emphasizes research and training for academic and industrial researchers as well as graduate students. The program also is intended to strengthen New Jersey's base in molecular toxicology, biomaterials, cell separation technology, and clinical pharmacology and metabolism. The goal is for new advances in biotechnology and biomedical science to be rapidly transferred to industry. New Jersey, sometimes referred to as the medicine chest of the nation, is the home of many major U.S. pharmaceutical and chemical companies. The state government hopes that the advanced technology center in biotechnology will build upon this economic infrastructure and create new entrepreneurial biotechnology startup companies. According to Edelman, the larger companies will expand because New Jersey is a better place to do that kind of business. The small venture capital companies will tend to move in because it's a good environment.

New Jersey's other advanced technology centers should build upon the state's existing industrial strengths. A new, $7 million research facility will be constructed on the campus of the New Jersey Institute of Technology for the treatment and disposal of hazardous and toxic substances. A total of $9 million has been allocated for a Center for Ceramics Research at Rutgers University. A $6 million Center for Food Technology at Cook College/Rutgers will be constructed to research the chemical, biological and engineering aspects of food processing and storing. Future centers may be named by the new Commission on Science and Technology, the permanent commission that will implement all of the programs under the bond act.

If it follows the plans of the Governor's Commission on Science and Technology, the new Commission on Science and Technology (established in the Department of Commerce) will start three additional mechanisms; tech centers, innovation partnerships, and incubator centers. The tech centers are like extension services, supplying technical assistance, conferences, seminars, and continuing education programs to small- and medium-sized businesses. Three programs are currently operating in polymer processing, fishing and aquaculture, and information services/office automation. The commission will also implement innovation partnerships—grants of $10,000 to $250,000 to individual academic researchers performing applied research in emerging technologies that are of strategic importance to the New Jersey economy. These projects will receive matching funds from industry. Three partnerships have started in biotechnology, surface modification, and telematics (the marriage of computer and telecommunications technology).

Working groups are currently addressing research and development priorities in plastics recycling, aerospace, and photonics (optical and laser sciences). These groups may lead to the establishment of additional technology centers. The state also plans to supplement the supercomputer center that was established at the John von Neumann Center by NSF with $70 to $75 million over the next five years. The state will add $12 million to the center and help it in its plans to link twelve universities to the center's computers. The center is also receiving significant donations from industry. The Digital Equipment Corporation, for example, recently provided $8 million in equipment. Edward Cohen, director of the new commission, anticipates $120 to $125 million being available for the John von Neumann Center alone. The commission hopes to transfer some of this increased expertise in computers to the advanced technology centers and the tech centers. For example, it would like New Jersey to become the first state to use supercomputers for medical uses.

The Governor's Commission recommended the creation of a New Jersey Venture Capital Partnership to make equity investments in new technology-based companies operating in New Jersey. It also suggested a series of measures to facilitate banking in New Jersey for high-technology companies. The new commission will investigate these recommendations and the proposals to revamp the state's secondary and undergraduate education programs to train the future scientists and engineers in New Jersey.

Maryland

The State of Maryland has taken several bold steps to upgrade the University of Maryland's capabilities in biotechnology, providing unique types of linkages between city, county, state, and federal government agencies with private industry. The program began in September of 1983 when the University of Maryland's Task Force on High Technology and Biotechnology recommended establishing a center of excellence in biotechnology called the Maryland Biotechnology Institute. The Institute was established in the following January. According to Acting Director Rita Colwell, after a thorough study of the strengths of the university and needs of the state it became very clear that there was a need to strengthen molecular biology at the university.'The Institute, which unites the various activities in biotechnology taking place on campus, will add seventy-five new positions to the university over the next two years. It is centrally administered with a board of directors representing industry, the university, and government.

Baltimore County has a strong interest in the program because of its desire to attract new industry and strengthen its presence as an academic center. The county is investing about $20 million in land and buildings for the institute while playing a major role in the program's overall direction. Colwell estimates that the city of Baltimore will be investing a comparable amount and the state government will invest about $100 million over the next twenty years. The 1985 budget for the Maryland Biotechnology Institute was $2.575 million.

The Institute will administer four centers in diverse areas of biotech. The Center for Advanced Research in Biotechnology (CARB) is the first program to be established. It is being built under the administrative direction of Kevin Ulmer, formerly the director of advanced research for Genex Corporation. According to Colwell, CARB is intended to be a national center for biotech to provide cutting edge research in biomolecular modelling. Ulmer describes CARB as a novel collaborative forum for research—governmental, academic and industrial. He states that the administrators are trying to create a single new research facility where scientists from all these kinds of institutions can work together. CARB will not conduct research for products, but it will focus on developing technology, generating information with importance to industry, and providing facilities for graduate research and education. The center has chosen to focus on research concerning the three-dimensional structure of macromolecules, especially the analysis of their properties. In pursuit of this goal, CARB has agreed to share resources and conduct collaborative research with the federal government's National Bureau of Standards. Although this agreement caused some initial concern in Congress about the use of federal funding to benefit one local region, CARB's invitation for other state government centers to work with them and the Bureau has allayed these concerns.

Ulmer expects $1.4 million to be appropriated by the Bureau in 1986 for joint efforts with CARB. He believes that the Bureau is an invaluable resource in terms of scientists who are expert in chemical and physical measurement. Determining the three-dimensional structure of macromolecules is basically a measurement problem. The Bureau has unique capabilities that they can bring from outside the traditional biology area to this study. The Bureau is interested in the project because it will help them to establish standards of measurement that can be applied throughout the field of biotechnology. It has a precedent for this model of joint research and resource-sharing through the Joint Institute for Laboratory Astrophysics, a center managed by the University of Colorado. The CARB agenda includes a major program to study the growth of crystals; a program on X ray diffraction studies; research utilizing nuclear magnetic resonance technology; three-dimensional imaging of macromolecules; and the development of a microscope that uses quantum tunnelling to look at two-dimensional structures at the atomic level. The state has budgeted an annual amount of $1.5 million for CARB and has created eighteen new, related tenure track positions at the university.

One ambition of CARB is to attract major corporations and biotech specialty firms to conduct research with it and the Bureau of Standards. Although the University of Maryland has received expressions of interest by industry, no commitments have been made because the program lacked a technical focus. When Ulmer was hired, one of his first tasks was to identify and outline an area where CARB could achieve international recognition. A technical plan for CARB has already received enthusiastic endorsement by large corporations. Ulmer hopes to soon begin to structure collaborative arrangement programs with industry. He wants to establish a separate corporation with a board of directors comprised of corporations interested in participating with CARB in addition to representatives of the University of Maryland, Baltimore County, and the Bureau of Standards.

The Biotechnology Institute is opening separate centers in marine, agricultural, and medical biotechnology. The Center for Marine Biotechnology (COMB) will link the National Aquarium with the University of Maryland and Johns Hopkins. The governor budgeted over a million dollars for this effort in 1985. The Center for Agricultural Biotechnology will work with the United States Department of Agriculture in Beltsville, Maryland. Discussions have been conducted with

DuPont and Monsanto over possible collaboration with the center. The Center for Medical Biotechnology will be located in Baltimore on property that the city has made available to the university. The Governor of Maryland has approved a budget of $2.575 million for these two centers and the addition of thirty-six tenure track staff positions. In conjunction with all these research efforts in biotechnology, the University of Maryland intends to establish a center in bioethics where the social implications of this work will be debated.

Pennsylvania

Pennsylvania has one of the most vigorous industrial incentive programs, making use of its university resources and supplying liberal funding for new ventures. At the heart of Pennsylvania's efforts is the Ben Franklin Partnership Program. The program matches state funding with contributions from the private sector. Each of four advanced technology centers received initial funding of $250,000 in 1983. They matched this with $3 million in industrial money. The fiscal year 1984 program consisted of $18 million from the state out of a total of $73 million.

Some of this funding is spent on joint industry and university R&D programs in various high technology areas. The money is also applied to provide assistance to entrepreneurial efforts, including incubator space (inexpensive space for startups), entrepreneurial services that match local research with the needs of companies, and advisory programs that evaluate business plans. Some of the money in each center goes back to the universities and colleges through employee training and educational programs.

Dr. Walter Plosila of the state's Department of Commerce explains that the whole program is driven by the private sector. Unlike a number of states which are basically funding traditional R&D in the university (the professor gets something done and tries to find someone in the private sector to commercialize it) Pennsylvania has reversed the process. It requires the private sector and the university to work out a joint project initially, with the private sector firm putting in writing its commitment in dollars prior to state funding. Although great emphasis is placed on entrepreneurial startups, the advanced technology centers put about half of their effort into helping traditional indus-

tries, regardless of the product. For example, it has CAD/CAM with
the shoe and apparel industry and sensors with the steel industry.

The program ties Pennsylvania's research resources together with
the use of four designated advanced technology centers operating out
of some of Pennsylvania's finest universities. The Northeast Tier Advanced Technology Center is based at Lehigh, but it includes 50 other
private and public colleges and universities, 280 private sector firms,
and 40 foundations and other organizations. The Western Pennsylvania Advanced Technology Center is led by Carnegie-Mellon University and the University of Pittsburgh with seventeen other private academic institutions and over ninety-five private firms. Pennsylvania
State University is the location of another advanced technology center,
working with a network of 31 colleges and universities, and 162 private sector firms. The remaining center, the Advanced Technology
Center of Southeastern Pennsylvania, is located at University City Science Center, the oldest industrial park in the nation. The University of
Pennsylvania, Drexel University, Temple University, Thomas Jefferson University and Pennsylvania Hospital work with 30 colleges and
150 private-sector firms under this arrangement.

The Ben Franklin Partnership Program provides additional benefits
to complement state programs. As a result of passage of a $190 mil-
lion high technology economic development bond, the program has
received $23 million to be used in creating new opportunities aside
from the advanced technology centers. $17 million has been set aside
to develop a loan program for incubator space. These incubators are
typically refurbished buildings that provide a variety of small businesses with inexpensive rent, sharing of secretarial and other services,
sharing of equipment, and access to other entrepreneurial resources.
Pennsylvania claims to have had eighteen incubators in place by 1985,
probably the largest number of any state.

The rest of the $23 million is spent on grants to universities to
purchase engineering equipment and for the establishment of four regional seed venture capital investment funds. The Ben Franklin program stimulates entrepreneurial activity by providing three million dollars in seed capital for investment in startup firms. These firms typically
receive investments of $50,000 to $250,000. The program is given a
share of equity in return for its investment. The Ben Franklin Partnership also included $550,000 in grant money in 1984-1985 for helping

small businesses launch new technologies. Each participant receives a maximum of $35,000, a boost for young firms.

Pennsylvania has started some other programs to assist economic development through high technology. It has linked, for example, seventeen Pennsylvania Small Business Development centers to the advanced technology centers. These centers provide technical assistance to emerging firms. Pennsylvania has additional programs to foster technical training for jobs on a statewide basis. Finally, there are programs that study efforts to expand both domestic and foreign markets for high-technology-based businesses.

Pennsylvania measures its progress in developing the advanced technology centers in terms of employment and numbers of new firms involved with the program. Plosila explains that their objective is to create jobs. A progress report issued by the program concludes that in total, 2,042 jobs were created or retained with the assistance of the centers over the first twenty-two months of the program.

North Carolina

North Carolina's crown jewel for economic development is the Research Triangle Park, an immensely successful development that links participating companies with the state's finest universities.

North Carolina is a veteran and the envy among state development programs because of thirty years of planning and hard work. Recognizing that North Carolina was losing its leading graduates to the industrialized northern states, then Governor Luther Hodges decided in the mid-1950's to join the research forces of Duke University, the University of North Carolina at Chapel Hill, and North Carolina State University to defeat this disturbing trend. In complement to the newly emerging Research Triangle Park, the government established the Research Triangle Institute in 1959 to conduct contract research in the natural and social sciences. The park was unsuccessful in attracting tenants in its first few years. Governor Hughes eventually decided to market the park as an exclusive location for high-powered establishments conducting pure and applied research. The concept worked, attracting Chemstrand (now Monsanto) to buy a 100-acre research park plot. For six long years the park waited for another customer. Finally, IBM bought space for an expansion. Based upon "Big Blue" 's decision, other firms and government agencies decided to buy in. Today the park boasts such firms as Becton, Dickinson and Company, Data General, Northern Telecom, TRW, and Union Carbide. It is estimated that when current construction is completed, the park will have $1 billion in buildings, 23,000 employees, and a payroll of $600 million. The Research Triangle, named in honor of the points of the triangle formed by the universities, claims to have developed a community with the largest number of Ph.D.s in the nation.

When North Carolina measures its successes in attracting high technology, it can count on the Research Triangle Park and the Institute. Additional incentives for industry to locate there are the comparatively low operating costs. Only 7 percent of the work force is unionized. Finally, the state has been successful because it uses a long-term strategy for planning and marketing the concept of working in North Carolina. A staff of twenty-two industrial developers in the North Carolina Commerce Department pursues potential companies. The result is booming industrial growth in a state that was once known only for its tobacco and textiles.

Many states now offer some incentive to train workers. However, few states are as aggressive as North Carolina in this area. It promises to train all the workers needed for any company in the state that offers more than twelve new jobs. This great lure was promised first by then Governor Hodges in 1957. The policy helps keep the state's community college system vital and relevant to the overall economy.

North Carolina's high technology strategy has made an important contribution to the development of microelectronics and biotechnology. Both fields are encompassed in two separate technology centers.

The Microelectronics Center of North Carolina (MCNC) was founded in 1980 to integrate the various resources in the state for the rapid transfer of technology to industry. Started by the state's General Assembly with $43 million, projects cover semiconductor materials, devices and fabrication processes; integrated circuit design to support microelectronics applications; and computer science and computer-aided design. MCNC links Duke University, North Carolina A&T State University, North Carolina State University, University of North Carolina, the University of North Carolina at Charlotte and the Triangle Park's own Research Triangle Institute. Current industrial affiliates include General Electric, Airco Industrial Gases, and GCE/IC Systems. Affiliates that sponsor research get a first look at the research and obtain an option on licenses on a preferred royalty basis. The Board of Directors of MCNC includes the chancellors of the five participating universities, a representative of the Research Triangle Institute, six citizens appointed to one-year terms by the governor, and the president of the Microelectronics Center.

MCNC has as its goal the ability to manufacture the Ultra Large Scale Integration chip with over one million devices on a single chip. MCNC and the state won a major victory when the Semiconductor Research Corporation, a consortium of electronics firms and universities, decided to settle in Research Triangle Park and allow MCNC to manage a new thrust in manufacturing technology research. The Semiconductor Research Corporation has cited the existence of MCNC as a significant factor in choosing its new home.

MCNC has an industrial affiliates program that grants special privileges to corporations in return for a fee of $750,000 over a three-year period. Scientists from participating companies can work in MCNC. In addition, up to three staff members can go to MCNC for research and advanced degree education with all tuition paid by MCNC.

The North Carolina Biotechnology Center has made a name for itself since it was founded in 1981 by then Governor Hunt. It works to develop collaborative research beween universities and industry. According to Dr. Patterson, the Center's director, the Center's mission is to undertake a range of activities that will enhance the environment for research and development in the entire state of North Carolina, not just in the Research Triangle area. The Center sponsors grants for research and coordinates the state's biotechnology activities with an annual budget of $1.5 million. It also conducts seminars, conferences, workshops and other educational programs. One example is a consortium it is arranging and partially financing to build a plant molecular biology community among North Carolina colleges. It has gathered additional financial resources from Ciba-Geigy and R. J. Reynolds Industries to support a fellowship program in this field.

When DuPont searched for a place in 1983 to locate its Electronics Development Center, it examined fifty-six possible sites before deciding upon North Carolina. Its story confirms the attractions that the region offers to technology-oriented corporations. According to Gene Pettingill of DuPont, the firm visited thirteen areas before selecting North Carolina, examining livability, supply of people, educational opportunities, existing facilities and thirty-four other factors. Pettingill observed that Research Triangle Park had twenty years experience in building cooperation between business, government, and education. He learned that they really work together and support one another, and they're interested in developing their strength in microelectronics, as evidenced by MCNC. DuPont is happy with their Research Triangle Park location. Pettingill notes that taxation is reasonable, labor rates are moderate, and there's plenty of the Puritan work ethic.

New York

The state of New York is responding to the need to build a high-technology economy in a number of interesting ways. Its main proponent is the New York State Science and Technology Foundation, which offers four programs. The first, the Corporation for Innovation Development Program, was founded in 1981 to provide financial assistance to startup firms. It uses a revolving fund with $1 million from the Science and Technology Foundation and $1 million from the U.S. Economic Development Administration. This money is loaned out with the provision that the recipient company find $3 elsewhere for every $1 the state loans.

The Science and Technology Agency also directs a program that sponsors university research with industrial application jointly with industry. The R&D Grants Program funded nine initiatives in 1983, eight of which received matching funding from industry. For fiscal year 1984-1985 it distributed $25,000 each to eight research programs. The R&D Grants Program also provides a valuable referral service for projects it cannot fund. It refers these projects to over 3,500 businesses that might wish to finance them.

The heart of the Science and Technology Foundation's high-tech efforts is the Centers for Advanced Technology Program (CATs). With funds matched by the private sector, it has financed seven centers where government, industry and the university can interface for economic development. The centers include Columbia University (Computers and Information Systems); Cornell University (Biotechnology in Agriculture); Polytechnic Institute of New York (Telecommunications); SUNY of Buffalo (Health Care Instruments and Devices); SUNY Stony Brook (Medical Biotechnology); Syracuse University (Computer Applications and Software Engineering); and the University of Rochester (Advanced Optical Technology). Each program received approximately

$1 million in 1984-1985 for applied research, training of personnel, and, (with matching funding from industry) technology transfer from the university to the private sector. It provides small high-technology firms with access to equipment it could not afford to purchase and increases the spin-off of new businesses from university research. The Center for Biotechnology in Agriculture at Cornell, for example, provides research space and support for industrial scientists who partici-pate in basic research at the Center. It enables university scientists to consult with industry and assists developing companies in finding in-expensive incubator space. The Center invites participating companies to use its excellent facilities, take advantage of access to staff and students, and gain entree to faculty and scientific information from other national and international centers of excellence.

The New York State Science and Technology Foundation also spon-sors a Regional Technology Development Organization Program to help homegrown businesses accelerate their technology. Matching grants of up to $25,000 are made to local organizations that help these indus-tries. Most of these services provide information for local businesses in the form of reports or seminars. According to John DeFfigos of the foundation, assistance can come in a variety of ways. He illustrates the program's sponsorship of technology development centers. The or-ganizers tend to be industrial and university leaders. They cause inter-action between small firms, large firms, and universities. They help inventors get patenting and licensing work, they call upon technology-based firms and seek opportunities for helping them, either through universities or other programs. They also become brokers of goodwill and services. DeFfigos sees expansion of the Science and Technology Foundation's activist role in the coming years. With a new budget in excess of $20 million for both new and expanded programs, they have plans for incubators, a seed fund for product development, and a pro-gram for application of new technology to old processes.

California

California is well known as a center for both high technology and venture capital. Since the infrastructure for high technology already exists there, the programs that have been started recently by the state focus on developing university-industry ties. Joshua Newman of the state's Assembly Committee on Economic Development and New

Technologies says: "We have reacted to capital markets, we have a lot of entrepreneurs out here, and we seem to get facilities started if there's brainpower to start them, so we focus on brainpower—which is a form of technology transfer." The most ambitious of these programs, the Microelectronics Innovation and Computer Research Opportunities Program (MICRO), was established in 1981 for innovative research in microelectronics technology, its application in computer and information sciences, and its necessary antecedents in other physical science departments. It combines the resources of the entire state university system with the capital of private industry. Started with twenty-five companies and with additional participants joining each year, MICRO allows professors to obtain industrial sponsors who will support at least half the costs of a project that is mutually interesting. The professor submits the proposed project to peer review, then to an executive committee. A policy board governs the entire project. Its membership consists of three people each from industry, the state government, and the university.

In fiscal year 1984, forty companies participated and total contributions from the state and industry exceeded $3.9 million. MICRO awarded fellowships in excess of $200,000. The state doubled the program's budget for 1984-1985; contributing $4 million for eighty-nine projects. Industry paid $8 million to support these projects.

In addition to MICRO, the state has streamlined regulations to speed high technology development. Finally, California is encouraging the development of industrial parks. In January of 1984 it passed legislation allowing tax-exempt financing for the building of research-based parks.

Massachusetts

Massachusetts is in a similar position to California. Its strong technological infrastructure has attracted venture capital and a large number of high-technology ventures, particularly in microelectronics. The state is seeking to supplement this with support of basic education and a plan to tie universities in with industry. One strategy is to develop Centers of Excellence throughout the state. These centers are in the process of being established in marine science, photovoltaics, biotechnology and polymer processing. The biotechnology center will be located at the Bio-Technological Research Park, established by the

Worcester Chamber of Commerce and located near the University of Massachusetts Medical School in Worcester. It will coordinate a network of medical and biological institutes with industry. The state government is helping the Worcester Chamber of Commerce by actively marketing the park, perhaps the first industrial park devoted exclusively to biotechnology.

The heart of the industrial effort is the quasi-public Massachusetts Center of Excellence Corporation (MCEC), recently created by the state legislature. A total of about $2 million, or about $500,000 for each center, has been appropriated for the 1986 fiscal year. Each center of excellence is run with an individual technology board composed of experts from industry, education, and government. The board will pass on proposals for cooperative research ventures. It is expected that some of this government money will be matched by private dollars.

In the polymers area the MCEC is trying to unite the more mature plastics industry with small, new firms in supporting a productivity center that would tie in with the resources of the University of Massachusetts and the University of Lowell. According to Phoebe Kent of the state's Executive Office of Economic Affairs, they are trying to draw in far more of the mature plastics industry with the University of Massachusetts and, in a more applied manner, at the University of Lowell. "They are setting up a productivity center there with money that we helped them secure through the legislature. That will help them to see ways in which they can rethink where they're going." MCEC hopes to draw upon the large research and development facilities of General Electric and Monsanto in founding the center and supplement these resources through state funding. The Executive Office of Economic Affairs has also established the Massachusetts Technology Park Corporation to create a statewide network of facilities for science and technology education. The first center is a $55 million microelectronics center. Half of the money will be provided by the state, and half will be provided by industry.

Michigan

Michigan has developed a state program that promises to revitalize its older manufacturing industries, especially the ailing auto industry. The Industrial Technology Institute has been started by the Governor's High Technology Task Force to improve and promote industrial automation. Six laboratories have been constructed; they are devoted 25 percent to pure research, 25 percent to applied research, and 50 percent to developing prototypes and equipment to implement applied research. One focus of the research is to develop the factory of the future.

In addition to the Industrial Technology Institute, Michigan has established two other centers of excellence, the Michigan Biotechnology Institute and the Metropolitan Center for High Technology. The Metropolitan Center encourages the development of incubator environments, special industrial training, and the enhancement of R&D capabilities.

There is no doubt that these new federal and state technology development programs will change the landscape of American industry. The demand for cooperation between government, the universities, and industries is quite high. Positive incentives have been built into many of these programs to help the cooperating institutions maintain their identities while building tomorrow's high-tech economy.

6   Pro-competitive Research: A New Way to Do Business

A quiet revolution is taking place in the way many high-technology companies go about the business of research. It challenges the common free-market philosophy where each company keeps its secrets to itself and competes fiercely, often duplicating the competitor's research results. The challenge is pro-competitive research, the attempt by companies in a given industry to pool some of their research resources to conduct research in common. This activity is sparked in part by America's growing recognition of competition from Europe and especially Japan, where the government oversees collaboration and technology sharing among competitors.

Perhaps the most striking of these collectives is the Microelectronics and Computer Technology Corporation (MCC), a for-profit corporation in Austin, Texas, formed by thirteen shareholder companies from the allied computer-based industries. Brainchild of Control Data's chairman, William C. Norris, MCC is under operating control by Admiral Bobby Inman, former assistant director of the Central Intelligence Agency and a man who can keep secrets. His experience at the National Security Agency prepared him for the job, since "I had a lot of years of experience in getting people to work together who really didn't want to but knew they had to." The heart of MCC is a research program that runs $50 to $100 million per year with 325 employees and 200 researchers, 100 with Ph.D.s. Sixty percent of these researchers are hired by MCC and 40 percent are loaned by companies.

How did such a consortium start? According to Inman, there was a need for some type of program as early as 1968, when the United States experienced a substantial drop in graduate students in science and engineering, due in part to a cutback in support by the Department of Defense beginning in 1963. It took the threat of Japanese domination of the computer-related industries to spur competitors to take the risk of sharing information. The United States industry reacted with shock when in 1981 the Ministry of International Trade and Industry in Japan announced that it would sponsor a program in computer technology that was twice that of their successful semiconductor program of 1974–1978. According to Inman "this caused medium and small-sized United States computer and semiconductor firms to say that they could not individually afford the volume of research nor attract the quality of talent for the number of years that would be necessary to accomplish a breakthrough."

MCC includes four types of programs, each of which lasts six to ten years: packaging; software technology; VLSI/computer-aided design; and advanced computer architecture. Each shareholder participates in at least one of the programs for at least three years; each is expected to contribute scientists to the program. The company raised money by selling its shares at $150,000 each to originators of the plan. New shares can be bought for around $250,000. In addition, each company invests between $1 and $4 million per year for research projects. Participants receive about 70 percent of the royalty income as 30 percent is held by MCC. The rules governing the research are very clear: the research must be so basic that a product can't be envisioned. Eighty-five percent of the researchers are from industry and only 15 percent are from academia. Inman was worried at first that participants wouldn't contribute their best researchers. "I wasn't going to run a turkey farm where they dump people whom they want to get rid of." He's satisfied now with the level of researchers being contributed to the program.

Why are there no antitrust problems concerning the formation of MCC? There are no guarantees against companies carving up markets with the technology, so the program will be watched closely. The Justice Department has reviewed the scheme and approved it. Instrumental in MCC's safety is the passage in 1984 of the National Cooperative Research Act (NCRA), which made it less rewarding for companies to file nuisance suits under the allegation of antitrust problems. Inman sees the NCRA as a recognition that "with a decreased pool of talent and given the scale of competition internationally, we've got to do a more effective job of housing the talent that's created. We can't have them scattered across a whole range of competing industries, each recreating the same basic technology. You'll never get any focus on the long-term leaps.'' The arena of the international marketplace is the background for pro-competitive research. Groups like MCC do not cut down on competition; they intensify the competition, bringing it on at a level higher than before, and hopefully higher than the level of success among Japanese manufacturers.

This is a trial period for the shareholders. They don't know how much more to invest because they don't know the returns from such a consortium. Not all observers are convinced that the research pattern is a safe one. Michael Borrus, an economist at the University of California, Berkeley claims "I think the dangers of market sharing emerging from MCC are very high and in the end you might find coming out of MCC some set of market sharing arrangements between those firms." This would be a violation of antitrust laws, although the NCRA loosened restrictions considerably. One expert on NCRA, attorney Paul J. McGrath, says that as a result of the law, it is very unlikely that any research and development venture could be sued unless it turned out to be a cover for price fixing or some marketing conspiracy. NCRA requires that joint researchers file with the Department of Justice and the FCC indicting formation of the venture. It limits damages from suits to single damages; before the law it was more attractive to sue because a plaintiff could collect triple damages. McGrath does not feel that antitrust laws per se have had much influence in preventing joint research ventures. He claims that to some extent the unease that is inherent in setting up joint ventures resulted in some finger pointing at the antitrust laws, using the antitrust laws as a scapegoat. NCRA made that difficult to do.

Parallel to the MCC effort is the Semiconductor Research Corporation (SRC), a group of semiconductor and computer equipment companies who sponsor research at selected universities in the United States. There is overlap in the board of directors of SRC and MCC, a sign that both efforts are complementary. The purpose of the organization is to improve the training of university personnel in the semiconductor field and to raise the level of science in this field so that American semiconductor companies can compete on a higher level. It currently holds fifty-three contracts with thirty-five universities with a budget of $16 million. Its goals include a $100 million annual budget; the development of a university/government/industrial research center; the integration of the information technology research domain; United States domination of information technology; and support of 1,000 graduate students and 300 faculty members.

Like MCC, SRC was founded after it was realized that Japanese corporations threaten to dominate their field. Its qualifications include the requirements that funding companies be controlled by Americans, perform a substantial program of research in the United States, and have its base of operations in the United States. SRC's goal is to promote, coordinate, conduct and sponsor research among these companies. The research is all conducted by university professors and graduate students, but SRC allows participants to send workers on campus to discuss the progress of the work. In addition, SRC-sponsored universities have regular seminars for members. Research applications are received from the universities. SRC has a Technical Advisory Board (consisting of representatives of government and universities as well as of industry) which monitors the progress of the program.

Cornell's Nowell MacDonald, in charge of SRC's presence on campus, speaks highly of the program but sees some inherent problems. The best form of technology transfer comes when personnel from the companies participate on campus or faculty go to the corporations to teach. However, it is difficult to get good people to do this because their time is tied up on their regular work. He praises the monthly seminars as "technology transfer presentations." On the whole he gives SRC high marks but states that it will take some time for the corporate environment of SRC to mesh with the realities of teaching and conducting research on campus.

William Howard of Motorola claims that the experience of starting SRC in 1982 helped clear the way for MCC. He and Inman do not see the two groups as competitive in any way. SRC is non-profit, university-based, and directed toward scientific development. MCC is interested in technology development with very specific projects. The fact that there is overlap between companies indicates just how desperate semiconductor companies feel about their futures. Says Howard: "Just look at the size of the Sumitomo group and the Mitsubishi group. We were forced with a threat that is very powerful and very directed." SRC's director, Larry Sumney sees SRC as a national industrial self-help effort to look at some of the long-term things that would help the semiconductor industry survive; to some extent there is a national unity drive behind it, he believes. In similar times of crisis this country has reliably turned to the university system several times in the past. The Japanese can't compete at this level because their universities are not research organizations; they concentrate on education and training, while the research is conducted in the corporations. Motorola's E. David Metz adds that SRC "is not directed toward the specific applicable technical output short term. It's really to improve the competence of the university."

Another new pro-competitive research organization is an alliance of Department of Defense contractors called the Software Productivity Consortium (SPC). It is modelled largely after MCC, conducting its own research in-house with a permanent staff; approximately 20 to 30 percent of the staff will be on loan from participating companies. Unlike MCC, participants have access to all the projects being funded. SPC, which is too young to have a research staff, will conduct its research through an R&D limited partnership. This allows them to take tax credits of roughly 90 cents on each dollar if the research can be taxed against profits. Each company should be able to bill back its payments to the government as part of its research costs for defense contracts; it is buying the research product for use in its contracted business. All of the research will be conducted on developing software that can be used for defense purposes. The first project will be a reusable software tool which will act as a library for contractors seeking specific software that has already been developed elsewhere. Like MCC, sponsoring companies get a three-year exclusive license on all tools and techniques produced. SPC will employ a staff of 200 and annual funding of about $50 million.

SPC is only one of a number of research consortia that have recently sprung up with the blessings of the Reagan administration, most especially through the office of D. Bruce Merrifield, Assistant Secretary for Productivity, Technology and Innovation in the United States Department of Commerce. Merrifield is convinced that the health of this country is going to depend upon the growth of these research consortia. He meets with leaders in various industries, the CEOs of competing firms seated in the same room, and tries to convince them to upgrade their technology base through use of the R&D limited partnership. He claims to have been successful with some very old industries, including the cement industry.

Spurred on by Merrifield's office and under the protection of the

National Cooperative Research Act (NCRA), a number of joint ventures have recently formed. One of the most interesting and controversial is the International Partners in Glass Research. This is a joint venture including United States, West German, Japanese, Canadian, English, and Australian glass manufacturers. They have committed $5 million over three years to conduct basic research in universities. Their goal: to develop glass that is ten times stronger and half the weight of current glass. This is an industry-wide attempt to overcome competition from plastics and paper container manufacturers.

Another joint research project is in optoelectronics devices. Managed by Battelle Memorial Laboratories, it will focus on developing basic manufacturing technologies for low-cost mass production of components. Techniques, materials, testing procedures and standards will be developed. These components are involved in switching, splitting, amplifying and modulating light signals, and processing optical data. The major problem the consortium will address is the alignment and bonding of fibers and optical components under mass production requirements. There is a need to build tiny robotic components which, guided by computers, will perform this task. "What we envision is a bit like designing the skilled assembly worker into the material," says Robert Holman, the program director. The research will be applied to computer systems, telephone systems, local area communications, factory floor process control, military systems, and process control systems in hazardous environments.

A smaller but important new project is the Center for Advanced Television Studies (CATS), the brainchild of top executives at ABC and Ampex. The consortium includes all three networks plus seven other companies involved in the television industry. They are pooling funds to support both consumer and technological research, focusing on enhancing efficiency of television signal transmission for improved sound and picture quality. CATS intends to facilitate the continuing education of scientists and engineers in industry, using a three-year, $2.7 million project at MIT as a springboard. The MIT program is called the Advanced Television Research Program (ATRP). The university maintains all patent rights but the companies get nonexclusive licenses to their work.

The goal of CATS will be the high-tech enhancement of the industry to, once again, stave off Japanese competition. Home Box Office's Horowitz claims CATS is trying to come up with a focal point for the

United States to pool efforts and come up with the next generation of television transmission that may be better geared to being competitive with computer processing than with the brute force method that the Japanese are trying to promote. The competition centers around machine standards as well as quality of transmission. One of the principal areas is consumer research, going to the man on the street to see how many lines on the television screen he would want to see. This will be paralleled with research on the ability to use computers to interpolate video pictures.

Bellcore is another example where competing companies pool their research funding. With an enormous research budget of $880 million to support 7,200 technical personnel, it serves as a research arm for seven telephone companies. Bellcore was created after the divestiture of AT&T; many of its employees originally worked with Bell Labs. Bellcore is a supporter of the Microelectronics and Computer Technology Corporation (MCC), participating in the advanced computer architecture and software technology segments of the program. In 1985 Bellcore established a major new laboratory at Rutgers University for research on modifying surfaces in the areas of semiconductors and communications technology. Some of Bellcore's general research areas include packet switching, fiber optics, networking, and sophisticated computer technology. Bellcore is a subsidiary of the seven companies that own it. It will analyze products that vendors are trying to sell to operating companies, conduct laboratory tests of components used by the companies, and check the quality of the suppliers' manufacturing processes. It acts as a giant consultant and joint research enterprise for the phone companies. Even though some of these companies are competing in the field for business, they manage to put aside their competition for joint research.

The electric power industry sponsors a great deal of pro-competitive research. Since electric power companies are regulated monopolies, competition is not a problem to be faced. The Electric Power Research Institute (EPRI) has been operating since 1973, when the Justice Department gave it clearance. EPRI's Richard Rudman explains: "The scope of the program covers anything of technical interest to the utility industry, from the processing of coal, new types of generation facilities, to new, improved transmission and distribution and improved ways of using electricity." A very strong theme that runs throughout the program is environmental concerns. With a budget of $350 million and a staff of 750, EPRI's research goals are much broader than the in-house research goals of member companies. It has a planned R&D budget of $2.1 billion from 1985–1989, some of which is spent on university research contracts. Including cost-sharing and co-funding, the R&D budget amounts to $3.6 billion for those years. The technology transfer to its 500 participating companies is very significant. Over 900 reports and 200 seminars are sponsored each year.

Following on the heels of EPRI is the Gas Research Institute (GRI), modelled partially after EPRI and formed in 1977. GRI is an organization of natural gas pipeline and distribution companies. Most of the R&D results are not translated into the member companies but into the suppliers to these companies. GRI plans, manages and develops financing for a cooperative R&D program in supply, transport, storage and end-use of gaseous fuels. With a 1986 R&D budget of $137.8 million, it sponsored over 300 research contracts. There are four new areas of basic research that interest GRI: methane reaction science; gas flow research; exploratory concepts; and biotechnology applications.

In contrast to other industries, interviews with top officials in the chemical and drug industries indicated that there was no pull to pool efforts in joint R&D programs under the limited partnership scheme. The companies are seemingly too competitive and do not feel the force of competition from Japan and Europe as the semiconductor companies do. However, the chemical industry does participate in some joint research and support research at universities through the Council for Chemical Research (CCR), an alliance of thirty-six member companies and 136 universities that serves as a technology transfer organization. CCR gives unrestricted grants to member universities. It also sponsors a program to bring one hundred assistant professors from member universities to companies to give seminars and explore areas of mutual interest. CCR also distributes information to member companies that publicizes the areas of interest of the top young researchers. The council has another program in which it encourages young professors to spend several weeks at a time in industrial laboratories, where they present short courses on their work.

The chemical industry also pools funds for research on toxicology of commodity chemicals through the Chemical Industry Institute of Toxicology (CIIT). Founded in 1974 and employing a staff of 106, CIIT does toxicity studies, predicts human risk of chemicals through both epidemiologic and lab studies, develops animal and human model

systems for predicting risks, elucidates mechanisms of chemically in-
duced toxicity, develops risk assessment procedures for information
about mechanisms, trains toxicologists, and provides information to
society on the scientific basis for evaluating toxicology. Despite the
fact that CIIT depends upon industry for its funding, it stresses independence in its research. The 1984 research budget was about $4.6
million. CIIT also supports predoctoral and postdoctorate fellowship
programs in toxicology for those who attend graduate school at Duke,
Vanderbilt, University of North Carolina-Chapel Hill, or North Carolina State College. In addition, it sponsors a visiting scientist program
in which a scientist from a university, government, or industry can
work at CIIT for six months at a time.

What is the meaning of all of this cooperation? Simply put, America
is adjusting to a new phase in business development. It can no longer
rely upon the old forms of competition in major industries. Even the
steel companies are beginning to conduct cooperative R&D. Can industry cooperate without carving up markets? There's no reason why
it shouldn't be able to if certain precautions are in place. Cooperative
research carried out by groups like MCC is a form of protection against
foreign competition. The secrets are kept for three years by MCC and
its affiliate companies to avoid the Japanese method of lifting technology out of the United States. Perhaps SRC and MCC are models that
will keep the universities free to disseminate knowledge; to protect our
technology, the alternatives to these research cooperatives might be to
stop the free flow of knowledge out of the university, something that
most universities would fight vigorously.

Most of the above-mentioned programs rely upon the actual exchange of personnel. Unfortunately, a company is unlikey to risk its
best researchers on speculative projects where a bottom line is not
visible. On the university side, it's difficult if not impossible to get
good researchers to give up their sabbaticals to teach in industry what
they have been teaching in the university. The alternative to personnel
exchange, the seminar, is helpful but is no substitute for having an
individual train and work actively on the project.

The Reagan administration's support of the R&D limited partnership and its activist stance are departures for an administration that
promotes a laissez faire philosophy. The government is playing an
active role in developing the R&D limited partnership. It is part of an
industrial policy, although the Reagan administration shies away from

calling it that. It's important to remember that in programs like SPC the taxpayer is paying the actual research cost because the R&D is billed back to the government. In programs like EPRI, the customer pays the research bill through a surcharge system. Pro-competitive research like this lies in the hands—and the wallets—of the citizens.

Questions should be raised about MCC's ability to conduct research when it cannot envision a product. It is hard to believe that the basic research it is conducting will not yield some predictable products. Like biotechnology, the microelectronics researcher travels a short distance from the "R" to the "D."

If groups like MCC and SRC start in part because of a lack of trained personnel in their fields, it is the government's responsibility to examine the supply and demand of researchers on campus. This is an area where the National Science Foundation (NSF) can make a real contribution. Its recent announcement of centers for supercomputer and other major research is a real help. This will provide opportunities for better training of scientists and engineers, but will it increase the interest of undergraduates in pursuing these related professions?

The wave of pro-competitive research does not fit in with the standard way of doing business, but it should be encouraged. The American economy depends upon its technological edge to remain strong in world markets. Pro-competitive research does not eliminate competition; it simply raises the stakes. It should be encouraged as an efficient way to organize some of the best minds of society to work together.

7   The Technology Transfer Specialists

Two recent phenomena point toward the emergence of entrepreneurial science as a major element in today's business climate. The emergence of special technology transfer companies—firms that specialize in selling technology instead of products—demonstrates how rich the university environment is for the commercialization of science. The other feature is the establishment of new ventures by university administrations.

One of the most successful technology transfer companies is University Patents, Inc. (UPI). It specializes in evaluating university research, bringing about its commercialization and protecting the rights to any resulting product. A public company, UPI is the exclusive agent for commercializing technology from seven major universities. In addition to patent management, UPI establishes spin-off companies from the technology of its clients. Included in the list of spin-offs is University Genetics, University Optical Products and University Communications; University Genetics is also a public company with five subsidiaries but University Patents owns 62 percent of the stock.

When UPI represents a university, it employs a total patent management system. The company takes a percentage of the licensing fees for its income. The institutions that are currently under exclusive contract include the Medical College of Pennsylvania, New York University, Princeton University, the University of Pennsylvania, the University of Illinois, the University of Arizona, and the University of Colorado. These institutions inform UPI when one of their investigators has a patentable invention. UPI meets with the inventor and develops a business plan for commercializing the invention. The com-

pany may raise money to start a corporation or it may supply money
to the inventor to continue his work. UPI also works out an agreement
with the administration of the university. Finally, the company manages licenses and protects its patents.

One example of UPI's successful operations centers around the work
of Marvin Caruthers, a University of Colorado scientist who performed breakthrough research on the synthesis of DNA. He developed
a "gene machine" that custom-synthesized DNA for work in diagnostic probes and pharmaceutical manufacturing. UPI has represented his
work, acting first as a negotiator with the university to determine proprietary rights and later with companies that make products from the
technology. Thanks to UPI the invention was licensed to Applied
Biosystems and SmithKline Beckman. UPI also acted as venture capitalist, supplying $160,000 to Dr. Caruthers' lab to support his re-
search. In addition, the company served as patent manager, filing twenty-
nine domestic and foreign patents for his work. UPI has enforced the
patents through filing a patent infringement suit. Finally, the company
has worked with licensees to the patents to hasten the commercialization of products. Says Dr. Caruthers, "UPI has done an outstanding
job of patenting, licensing, and protecting the invention."

In another case, UPI helped a scientist found his own small company that focused on commercializing a single technology. Gebhard
F. B. Schumacher invented a plastic syringe that helps women determine their fertility by measuring vaginal fluid volume, known to increase during ovulation. UPI filed the patent and created a startup joint
venture company, OB/GYN Concepts Ltd., that concentrated on the
technology's development. UPI received equity in the company for its
efforts and shares royalties on sales with the university. According to
Charles Root, the president of OB/GYN Concepts Ltd., UPI did all
the patent work including the legal aspects.

A. Sidney Alpert, the president of University Patents, explains that
three criteria are used when evaluating technology: its patentability,
the value of the technology, and its marketability. Since the firm deals
on an exclusive basis and spends a significant amount of time and
involvement in evaluating technology on campus, it looks for a particular configuration in a university. A candidate university would spend
about $25 million or more annually on research. The university has to
have a patent policy in which the university takes title to their inventions. Finally, the university should have a capable administration that

doesn't allow the professors to "go over the transom" with their inventions.

UPI is currently operating at a net loss, a condition which is due to its acceptance of all the operating costs of its subsidiary, University Optical Products Co. However, it increased its revenues from technology management by $351,000 from 1984 to 1985.

In contrast to UPI, Research Corporation is a non-profit organization that manages patents and licenses from universities on a non-exclusive basis. It offers business support services to startups developing out of the laboratories of professors at universities. It also negotiates licensing agreements and provides legal protection against patent infringement.

The foundation competes indirectly with UPI; however, its purpose is different. Founded in 1912 by philanthropist and inventor Frederick Gardner Cottrell, Research Corporation was started as a public service to help university professors commercialize their inventions. It has non-exclusive agreements with nearly 300 institutions. Research Corporation uses its staff of patenting, technology, and legal experts to evaluate an invention's commercial usefulness without charge to the inventor. It may help the scientist raise money to commercialize the invention. However, its main functions are in the management of the patent and the licenses. Research Corporation normally takes 40 percent of the royalties and returns 60 percent to the university, which in turn distributes an average of 15 percent to the inventor. The foundation works from a $50 million endowment. In 1984 it returned approximately $7 million in royalties to universities and non-profit research institutions.

The money that Research Corporation takes in is used in part to sponsor two grants programs with a combined budget of close to $3 million. The Cottrell Research Grants Program supports basic research in the physical sciences at private graduate and all public academic institutions. The Cottrell College Science Grants focus on research in the natural sciences at private, predominantly undergraduate colleges.

Stevenson Bacon explains that there is a need for Research Corporation because the universities with small patent administration offices don't have the contact with industry necessary to make good deals. For example, they tend not to understand the factors involved in setting royalty rates. Sometimes they don't pay attention to the need for diligence clauses that specify that the manufacturer will adequately produce and sell the product. Administrators at universities tend not to know how to protect their inventions in the Common Market and the Far East. One third of Research Corporation's patent royalties come from these sources. Using the guideline of $1 million in research funds for each invention, Bacon states that many universities find that the patent administrator's office will not pay for itself.

It is the lack of know-how and the lack of manpower that cause universities to call upon Research Corporation. The company has recently had between 300 and 400 disclosures per year. Its royalties are, according to Bacon, about $10 million per year.

Research Corporation doesn't charge for its initial patent evaluation. The firm expends about $50,000 to protect the invention worldwide and a similar sum to license the invention. Because of these figures, Research Corporation has to turn down many inventions. This has damaged their reputation on campus to some extent. Research Corporation was also reputed at one time to be too casual, not pursuing inventions as actively as it could have done. The firm has made concerted efforts to counter this charge by playing a more proactive role on campuses. According to George Stadler at Research Corporation, the organization is seeing an increasing number of disclosures and a higher royalty income over the past few years. Stadler sees university patent administrators who tried to make it on their own coming back to Research Corporation because they don't have the technical breadth or experience in negotiating agreements with the different industries. Research Corporation is now trying to counter the notion that the only ways of handling the technology are to do it in-house or turn it over to somebody else. By trying to coordinate with the administrator's office and contribute what each can do best to the relationship, the chances of maximizing a university's potential are higher. It also educates the administrators about the commercial potential of the university's technology.

There has been a definite growth in the sheer number of university patent administrators in the past decade. This may be partly due to the improved awareness of the potential of technology transfer out of the university. Increasing pressure from state programs and the change in the patent law in 1980 allowing universities to hold title to federally funded inventions helped commercialize the university. The emergence of the federal government's Small Business Innovation Research (SBIR) program stimulated universities to think of ways of using SBIR funds to test new product concepts. The increased presence of venture capitalists on campus and the use of biotechnology as an example of successful technology transfer provided added impetus for administrators to pursue commercial interests. These trends are confirmed by the growth of the Society of University Patent Administrators, which now gets 200 to 250 administrators to attend its conference. Conferences increasingly cover the licensing and marketing of patents.

As technology transfer services grow, alternative arrangements are being explored by universities to manage their own technology. There is a trend now for universities to get involved in starting up companies either directly through their offices of technology licensing or indirectly through non-profit foundations. One of the leading universities in this area is the University of Utah, which has founded thirty startups in the past five years. The university holds 10 percent of equity from these companies through the University of Utah Research Foundation. According to J. Winslow Young, director of the Office of Patent and Product Development, the university has a policy of not participating in the management of the companies or representing itself on the boards of directors.

Young realizes that there is great potential for conflicts of interest in establishing new ventures, but he uses three mechanisms to deal with the problem. First, the licensee agreement requires that the company monitor its own employees, including any Utah professors, for conflicts of interest. Secondly, if there seems to be a conflict of interest, the responsible parties are required to file with the secretary of state. Finally, if a company plans to conduct research on campus, the research is monitored by a separate entity called the engineering experiment station, which acts as the principal investigator. It monitors the contract and reports all findings to the company.

How sucessful will the university companies be? It's too early to tell. Several additional companies started by the university have failed. Young expects a high rate of failure for these speculative ventures, anticipating that only about half a dozen companies will reach sales of $20 million or more. Young claims that it's a shakeout period, but in another ten years the university will have an outstanding success. All he needs is a 10 percent success rate, he claims, to be competitive with Stanford, MIT, and Harvard.

Young has an innovative idea for stimulating new ventures that he would like to test. He wants to spend about $20,000 each for support of postdoctoral students who submit a project to the university for technical and marketing analysis. As the research progresses, marketing analysis will proceed. Young sees this as a valuable way to support postdoctoral students who need research money as well as another chance to stimulate the formation of new ventures. These new companies can find space in the Utah Innovation Center, an incubator facility originally set up through the National Science Foundation which is run by the university and now supported by private capital.

Young uses Evans and Sutherland, a computer graphics corporation, as an example of the type of success that campus-based companies can bring. The company was started by two researchers, one of whom was later appointed chairman of the university's computer science department. Assisted by graduate students at Utah, Evans and Sutherland begin to develop and patent fundamental work involved with computer-aided design. Both founders are now adjunct faculty members who located their company in the Utah Innovation Center with a staff of 750 employees. Their current chief products are computerized simulators used in jet pilot training, and computers and terminals for engineering design stations. Unfortunately for the university, this highly successful company was founded before the university had a policy of working with new ventures on an equity basis. Evans claims that he would have been willing to give up 10 percent of the company to the university in the early years.

Baylor College of Medicine has taken a different route than the University of Utah, founding BCM Technologies as a private, for-profit entity. BCM specializes in starting new companies based upon Baylor technologies and managing the licensing of the technologies. The company was founded in October 1983 after several years of debate over how to manage the results of a research and development budget of over $70 million. BCM subsequently hired William T. Mullaney, an executive who had ten years of experience in marketing at Johnson & Johnson, as president of the company. When BCM called for proposals from the faculty, over one hundred proposals were screened and twenty-five were selected. BCM then called in a marketing consulting firm to do a technical market analysis. This brought the candidates down to ten projects. A scientific advisory board was started with the chairmen of nine departments. The board reviewed the projects for technical feasibility. From this work they have developed one company that has started marketing products, another one with the investment in place through venture capital, and another one with Eli

Lilly backed by $1.5 million. The Eli Lilly project involves using Baylor technology on one of their therapeutic products, for which BCM will receive a licensing fee and a royalty.

How was Baylor able to start a for-profit company? One reason is the entrepreneurial spirit of Houston, Texas, where it is located. Another reason is that Baylor is a private, independent medical college. It has no history or philosophy departments to challenge whether academic freedom would be compromised by commercialization. The program is extremely generous to its scientists, offering them a 50 percent equity in the new company. BCM does all of the work in capitalizing the project by talking to investment bankers and private investors. BCM also does all of the business plans for the new companies. It tries to keep the scientists' involvement at this stage at a minimum, preferring that they concentrate on the science. BCM will be an interesting model to follow over the coming years. It will be particularly important to note whether its high rewards to the scientists will change the focus of research there.

Case Western Reserve University (CWRU) has taken a similar approach to Baylor in setting up a company that will commercialize the university's research. According to Thomas H. Moss, Dean of Graduate Studies, since commercialization is a fact of life at the university, the key question is to manage it in order to meet all the kinds of constraints and goals that the university has rather than try to stop it from happening and then have it happen in a random and unpredictable fashion. Speaking of scientists who want to commercialize their research, he claims that if they had no framework in which to do it, the faculty members might not stay at the university and do the startup; he sees the program as valuable for retaining good faculty members. Through its subsidiary and through the dean's office the university has concluded over forty-five R&D licensing agreements and four new startups within the past two years. The university becomes part owner of the new venture but it does not play any management role. The company finds entrepreneurs who do the actual structuring of the new ventures. Moss explains that the main role that his office and the company play are to act as agents of technology transfer by whatever is the best means possible. He claims that it's not as if they have a strategy to do startups; they have a strategy that says they want to do technology transfer in whatever way that works. The company that participates on behalf of the university, University Technology, Inc. (UTI), also plays a role in educating people on campus about the benefits and options involved with technology transfer.

UTI is very much oriented into networking with city and state technology development programs. For example, it is involved with a venture capital fund called Cleveland Tomorrow, which can supply money for startups. CWRU is also a founder and participant in three technology transfer programs initiated by the Thomas Edison program, a state-funded entrepreneurship program which has received funding in excess of $32.4 million. CWRU participates in the Cleveland Advanced Manufacturing Program, the Edison Animal Biotechnology Center, and the Edison Polymer Innovation Corporation. All of the technology developed by CWRU is licensed through UTI. UTI will also go to companies to persuade them to license CWRU technology.

Why did CWRU go ahead and set up UTI rather than keep technology licensing within the university administration? Moss claims that there's no big deal about having a separate company. It's easier to have a separate entity which he can observe instead of having it as a half time function of an administrator. We disagree about the change. It is a major step for a university to set up a separate technology transfer corporation. This signals a major new commitment on the university's part to be entrepreneurial. Moss believes that the surge in technology for licensing is due in part to patent law changes enacted in 1980 that allow universities to hold title to patents for federally funded research. This means that universities suddenly are in a position to take a million dollar federal basic research investment and leverage it into a commercial venture for perhaps another few hundred thousand with an advanced prototype. The 1980 law was an important step taken by the government to encourage technology transfer.

When UTI commercializes this research it has several goals and incentives that differentiate it from a traditional venture company. It must work to fulfill faculty members that participate, making the commercialization process as enjoyable and headache-free as possible. UTI must also give preference to enhancing technology within the region, a promise that is backed by its participation in state and local technology development programs. It is interested in long-range constructive relationships with industrial sponsors or development of ventures that will pay off for the university in ways besides the ownership of equity. Finally, the reward structure of UTI reflects the university's commitment to not compromise longer-term rewards with short-term, up-front payments. UTI and CWRU are interested in forging a network of relationships that will pay off throughout the coming decade. In this sense, the university is acting as a prudent investment manager.

The University of Connecticut has also set up a company to commercialize its research but, unlike CWRU, its company is established to make a profit. Called the University of Connecticut Research and Development Corporation (UCRDC), it is wholly owned by the University of Connecticut Foundation. Since total university research budgets are approximately $45 million, there is quite a large potential for commercializing research. UCRDC has launched its first venture, Bio Polymers Inc., which specializes in manufacturing an adhesive based upon a gluey substance excreted by mussels. UCRDC gets a 10 percent equity position in addition to licensing fees and product royalties.

According to its president, Lyle Hohnke, a venture capital fund is being established at the university to provide a vehicle to finance startups. It will be capitalized by private investors and the University of Connecticut Foundation. The venture capital fund is a significant sign that the university is committed to playing the role of entrepreneur. This striking model of commercialization from the university would have been unheard of five years ago.

Like Baylor's BCM, UCRDC provides a neutral buffer between faculty commitments to the university and business activities related to commercialization of faculty research. The formation of UCRDC allows for greater flexibility in discussing deals with outside venture groups, private investors or large corporations than would otherwise be possible. Because the University of Connecticut is a state university, it would be constrained in its new venture development dealings without an organization like UCRDC; for example, it could not take equity in companies. Profits from UCRDC go back to the university to fund additional research.

The structure of UCRDC was established in October of 1984 after two years of intensive debate. Claims Hohnke,

We differ some from the Baylor model in the sense that our board of directors felt that we did not want to run the risk of outside influence by selling stock outside of the foundation. That is always an option down the road should capital become necessary. But for the first go-around all of our stocks are owned by the foundation versus the Baylor model where they do have some outside investors who, in the view of our board, could begin to influence the direction the marketing organ might have.

If universities follow the UCRDC model, they should also retain all of the company's stock. The university has other allegiances besides the profit motive. They have to retain faculty and maintain research excellence. For these reasons, the profit motive might necessarily be influenced.

One advantage of the UCRDC model is that it minimizes the possibility of direct university involvement in product liability lawsuits. As a result of UCRDC's independence, Hohnke has to negotiate with the university over rights to intellectual property. UCRDC does not have an exclusive arrangement with the university. This provides for extra flexibility in making deals. For example, it can attempt to create cooperative projects between University of Connecticut faculty and other researchers from universities or industry. This arrangement further serves the interest of technology transfer.

Washington University is also taking advantage of spin-offs from university research. It is supporting technology transfer through the formation of a venture capital fund and the development of a company designed to start new companies. The university has joined forces with Moshe Alafi of the Alafi Capital Corporation to start the Alafi-Washington Company (AW). Faculty members are free to commercialize through AW or seek venture capital funds elsewhere.

Unlike many of the other universities involved with technology transfer, Washington University doesn't allow its researchers to take equity or royalties involving a company; the equity and royalties are held by the university and resulting funds are distributed to the laboratory of the inventor. Duke Leahey of the licensing office believes that the lack of ownership of the company helps eliminate potential conflicts of interest when faculty members are involved in new ventures.

Stanford and Harvard have decided not to take equity positions in companies on a regular basis, citing conflict of interest problems. Stanford, according to Kathy Ku, associate director of technology licensing, has a practice of holding the patents and does not generally grant exclusive licenses to the startups in which faculty members hold equity or line management positions. We believe that Stanford might have to alter its position as other top schools make room for entrepreneurial science in the lives of its faculty members. The university does have a practice of granting exclusive licenses in areas where it believes that the technology can best be commercialized by one company. This happens especially in the pharmaceutical industry, where long periods of development and testing require that exclusive licenses be granted for the R&D to pay off.

Niels Reimers, director of technology licensing at Stanford, believes that the current practices are sufficient and there has not been a catalyst to make them consider becoming new venture specialists. He claims that the university has taken equity in selected cases in the past, but holding equity is a cause for concern.

Whether it's true or not, it could be perceived that the reason that you're licensing this new piece of technology to this company is because you have a significant equity position. Since most of our technology arises from public funding, we should go to the best companies, which may not necessarily be the one in which we have equity. This argues, I think, that the people who make endowment investment decisions should be quite separate from those who do the technology licensing.

Stanford has the obligation to best serve its interests. By funnelling technology to new ventures it creates, Stanford might have the opportunity to create the "best" companies for the technology. We suspect that Stanford is more concerned with its image as an independent institution than it needs to be. Perhaps its policy will change when other top schools take the entrepreneurial route.

At least one Ivy League university has differed from the stance taken by Stanford. William M. Jackson of the Brown University Research Foundation explains that two companies have been established by the university over the past year. One, Analytical Biosystems Inc., was founded by a Brown professor. Another is a non-profit database company that Brown has bought out and turned into a for-profit company.

Jackson doesn't appear to be concerned about the conflicts of interest that he admits are tied up in this venture.

We feel it's more appropriate to take action than to sit on the sidelines. Take action and keep your eyes open for potential conflicts of interest. Put everything out in the open and let people know what's there. . . . If anybody sees something that represents an action on the part of the university that acts as a conflict of interest, we'll try to correct it at that time. So far . . . nobody's raised any issues.

Jackson voices some strong opinions about other top schools which have not been involved in new venture development. Speaking of Stanford, he states

They've taken the position of "well, we don't feel we can avoid whatever conflicts of interest arise, so we won't try." We've taken the opposite position. We think we can deal with whatever conflicts of interest arise so we'll do it as a matter of philosophy. I don't think one side or the other is more right than the other. Unfortunately, when you take the position that Stanford takes, you never find out whether there are any conflicts of interest that can be dealt with.

One way of resolving potential conflicts, claims Jackson, is to have technology transfers and supplies negotiated with the company by someone in the university who is not an equity holder.

Countering the Stanford argument, Jackson states: "I would take the position that any university has some fiduciary responsibility to treat its assets so as to maximize the return on those assets. . . . I'd say that the conflict of interest is to underutilize the value of the assets available. That's a conflict of interest." Jackson points out that some technologies may be valuable but too young to be commercialized through licensing to a major corporation. "By having the courage of your convictions to actually begin a venture and get it funded and add value to it, you can increase the value of the return to the university."

How prevalently will entrepreneurial science be practiced at the level of university formation of new ventures? All signs indicate that this is rapidly gaining in popularity. Some schools will not consider it because of the image of conflict of interest. Other universities are well enough endowed so that there is less urgency to develop this new source of revenues. Nevertheless, the trend indicates that universities will become active investors in new technologies, creating yet another series of alliances with the United States business community.

This type of innovation should be strongly encouraged. It keeps the professors where they belong—in the university—while providing a badly needed source of revenues to the universities. The approach of setting these ventures up through independent non-profit or for-profit entities provides an arm's length relationship to the university that minimizes conflicts of interest. Since the university is not in the business of manufacturing products or developing technology, it is best if there is a close alliance between specialists in new venture development and university personnel engaged in technology licensing. Each university can determine how to best maintain that close alliance while remaining dedicated to the pursuit of knowledge.

Scientists should be encouraged to play a role in starting new ventures. It reflects well on the institution as well as the scientists if the ventures are successful. Schools like Washington University should allow their scientists to take equity and reap the royalties to their inventions. Conflicts of interest can be handled on a per case basis by a faculty committee. Entrepreneurial science should be encouraged in all its forms. It's healthy for the economy, for the scientists, and for the university administration.

8   The Financing of New Ventures

New ventures may be financed in four primary ways: through venture capital, investment by large corporations, public market financing, or the R&D limited partnership. The choice of funding depends upon the stage of the company and what it has to offer. The financing of the small company allows entrepreneurial science to move from the university to the small company and from the small company to the large company.

New ventures in biotechnology are financed in the early stages by venture capitalists. James Blair of Biotechnology Investments Limited (BIL) explains that venture capital financing takes place in any of four stages. In the seed stage, the company is paying an entrepreneur with an idea or a university with a strong patent position. It might invest in the range of $250,000 to $500,000 and expect to be paid 75 to 100 percent per year on their investment. The investment money is used to recruit other members of the management team and prepare the technology in anticipation of stage one financing. A stage one opportunity is one in which a startup has formed with a detailed business plan and a well-rounded group of executives that have been attracted to the venture so that there's a team in place to do the work. Biotechnology Investments Limited would expect a return of better than 50 percent for stage one. A stage two investment is one in which a management team has worked together for a good period of time and a product is developed and ready for initial product shipments but money is needed for expansion capital. BIL expects an annual return of better than 35 percent for their money. For third stage projects, BIL looks either for a company that has public market status or a leveraged buyout from a major corporation. The valuation of the business has to be established in the marketplace. BIL might come in if the stock were depressed and there were an opportunity to improve the company. BIL would expect about a 25 percent return on a stage three investment. Generally the company expects a lower rate of return on the higher-stage deals because their money is at risk for a shorter period of time. It might take seven to ten years for a seed deal to blossom, while it would take five to seven years for a stage one deal and three to five years for stage two. BIL has a policy of playing a very active role if not a board role in almost every one of their portfolio companies.

Blair sees that the universities have come a long way toward appreciating what the industrial role can be. He notes a relaxation of tensions in the deals where he has been active. He also sees a real change in the scientists who go to work for the companies.

What we found in a number of project areas is there was almost initial resistance to apply one skill set to what might be termed rather mundane kinds of assignments on the part of university-based researchers. But as they have gotten into the projects they see meaningful differences in what they've been asked to do or expected to do in a university environment. And they have no difficulty walking down both paths simultaneously because they see that the requirements and discipline are totally different.

The loosening of the university environment is exemplified by BIL's completion of a recent deal that gave the university equity in the company.

When evaluating a company for funding, Blair finds the biggest challenge is knowing how well the management team works together.

You can own in many cases considerably less than all of the stock, considerably less than half the stock in many cases, and so you can't really use the financial lever once a venture's been funded to control the entrepreneurs in the business. So really the team has to develop the ability to function on its own. Shaking out the team and making it function on eight cylinders is probably the most difficult part of new venture development.

What is new and significant about biotechnology venture funding is that venture capitalists are willing to invest money in ventures that they wouldn't have touched ten years ago because the companies are not actively manufacturing products and showing that they can operate in the black. The criteria for funding new ventures have changed. Venture capitalists are willing to fund these young companies because they are able to get a return on their investments through corporate funding or the public stock market. The stock market has been willing to fund these companies because of the tremendous promise they offer, even though many of the companies funded in this way had very small revenues.

Large companies can fund small companies in three ways: by purchasing equity, by acquiring the company, or by signing contracts for manufacturing and marketing or research. The acquisition of companies is a way of obtaining the small company's technology with no strings attached. Examples in biotechnology include the acquisition of Hybritech by Eli Lilly for $350 million and the acquisition of Genetic Systems by Bristol-Myers for approximately $297 million, or 28.3 million shares of Genetic Systems stock worth $10.50 per share in Bristol-Myers stock. The company can obtain access to the technology through joint ventures or other arrangements by which the small company hands over the manufacturing and marketing rights in return for money. This may be accompanied by a minority equity investment in the company to further align the interest of the small company with the large one. Cytogen, for example, recently accepted a $15 million equity investment by Eastman Kodak in addition to $6 million worth of research contracts.

All of the investment by corporations and public offerings fuel the venture capital process to continue to build on its successes. With increased ventured capital investment comes increased investments by large corporations, whereby more technology is transferred from the small company to the large corporation. As investments by large corporations increase, the small company is perceived by Wall Street to have more value, fueling investors in the stock market to pay higher prices per share or to buy new issues. Investment by large corporations adds credibility, leading to increased investment by additional companies in the small firm through joint ventures or research contracts. This credibility is very important with companies that have products that are several years away from the marketplace. Some of the more successful small companies know how to balance the venture capital funding with the investment by the large corporation to limit what they have to give up in equity or technology.

It is very important that a small company not give up too much of its technology. In biotechnology it is somewhat difficult to define the technology the small corporation is giving up to the large corporation because the technology is so new. For example, when interferon contracts were negotiated it was not known that there might be ten or twelve types of interferon. Another example is in the field of immunology where the terms of the contract are somewhat vague because the technology has yet to be developed. The small corporation must establish a good relationship of trust with the large corporation in these examples to be sure that the contract is carried out as both parties originally intended. There is a risk here that key personnel will leave over the course of several years and that the contract will be interpreted in a different light by replacement personnel.

In what order does the small company build itself up, both financially and in terms of technology? At Johnston Associates small biomedical and biotechnology companies are built with a combination of venture capital and corporate financing. The firm is unique in that it doesn't wait for business plans to be submitted by young companies. It forms its own companies with its own business plans, starting with a scientific breakthrough with technological promise. The first step is to find the key scientific personnel. In the case of Cytogen, Johnston Associates found Thomas McKearn, one of the top ten experts in the utilization of monoclonal antibody technology. The second step was to find a businessman/president who could assemble the management team: the vice president of marketing, the vice president of finance, and the vice president of corporate development. Johnston Associates raises the venture capital once the team is in place. Cytogen divides its technology according to the marketplace and licenses applications to corporate partners. The company retains a significant amount of the technology for development, manufacturing, and marketing in-house. Cytogen signed various agreements with American Cyanamid Company, Farmitalia Carlo Erba SpA, Eastman Kodak, Johnson & Johnson, COBE Laboratories, and BBL Microbiology Systems. The agreements all call for Cytogen to receive royalties from sales of specific linking technology developed by Cytogen for monoclonal antibodies. In some agreements, there is funding by the large corporation for research by Cytogen, with extra funding when certain scientific milestones are achieved. Although Cytogen is giving up rights to segments of its technology in the process, it intends to become a fully integrated pharmaceutical products company. It hopes to do this by retaining rights to its technology for linking antibodies to specific therapeutic preparations used in anti-cancer assessment and treatment. It will rely upon the investment by large corporations and the proceeds of its recent public offering of three million shares to finance itself while its proprietary products are under development and regulatory assessment.

Companies go public when they have the credibility of large corporations backing them and they time their appearance on the public market when technology stocks are doing well. Technology stocks do well when the overall market is doing well. The middle of 1986 was a good time for biotechnology stocks because biotechnology products were being marketed for the first time. Biotechnology stocks differ from other technology stocks because of the personal appeal of the products. Investors would rather support cancer cures than computers, given that all other factors are equal.

Another method of financing new ventures is the research and development limited partnership (RDLP). It can be started by forming a general partnership which manages the research and deveopment and adds limited partners—partners who are limited in that they are investors, not managers. The limited partners put up all the money for the partnership. The general partner is usually a part of the management of the parent company but it is legally separate from the company. The investment only covers the commercialization of a stated bit of research or clinical testing. The partnership is a tax write-off for the investor. If the research is successful, the limited partner shares in the royalties from the product, which is taxed as capital gains.

Limited partnerships originally evolved in oil and gas exploration where there was a high risk of failure. They became popular in biotechnology from 1982–1984 and subsequently fell out of fashion. Nevertheless, the success of some of the biggest biotech companies will depend in part upon the capital supplied by the limited partnership. At Centocor, for example, the company raised $23 million and pays out only a 7 percent royalty if the research is successful. The parent company takes no risk. If the research is unsuccessful, the parent company has no responsibility to the investor to pay him back. Unfortunately, there is a good deal of uneasiness on Wall Street about the R&D limited partnership. Some, like James Blair of BIL, feel they're appropriate only for the very sophisticated investor.

There are ways of financing new ventures that incorporate venture capitalism with new types of research and development agreements.

These are called blind pool partnerships; some of the biggest names on Wall Street have established them. Merrill Lynch has set up a separate company to sell these types of agreements. According to Bruce Shewmaker, president of Merrill Lynch R&D Management Inc., the partnership funds research primarily by entering into two contracts. First it establishes the "R&D contract where you have the budget, the buy-out arrangements, the cross licensing of the technology and all the other things that go into a normal R&D arrangement. We then go one step further and we enter into a second contract. This second contract is between the partnership and the individual engineers and scientists who are actually going to perform the work and remain as employees of the sponsoring company." The scientists sever their relationship in terms of patent assignments to their parent company; for that period of time when they work on the partnership's projects they actually assign those rights directly to the partnership. In exchange for that assignment, the partnership agrees to share with the scientists a portion of all royalty income received. This arrangement can result in very favorable tax treatment on the royalties for the investor in the partnership. Shewmaker believes this is important in that "we have, I think, for the first time brought the venture capital discipline to the funding of research and development in that we are providing an economic incentive for those people who create the business opportunities for all of us," the scientists. The scheme works for corporate research and university-based research, where the university allows their scientists to be directly compensated. By rewarding the scientist directly, the partnership may qualify under section 1235 of the tax code to treat all income as capital gains income without waiting for a holding period (as in other forms of the RDLP).

How enthusiastic is Shewmaker about this form of financing research? "I am absolutely convinced that we have a tool that for the first time allows us to directly reward those people who create the productivity enhancements and improvements and we may increase the competitiveness of US industry vis-á-vis foreign competition."

The effects upon society of these entrepreneurial efforts is varied. By shortening the time between research and development as is characteristic with biotechnology, you advance the product life cycle. You also make the products obsolete more quickly because of increased competition at the early research stages. In terms of the university, it is useful to think of the "university-industrial complex," a web of interrelationships that appears to strengthen both institutions. Entrepreneurial science is about taking chances. This risk taking feeds back to the university, where entrepreneurs fund risky research to yield risky technology. The entrepreneur has to have the intuition to envision a new product and a new market; he must also be able to communicate well with the president of the company, who in turn must have a handle on the technology. The university must be tolerant of efforts to commercialize research. Universities have become far more tolerant of venture capitalists over the past five years. Many have even started courses on entrepreneurship to encourage students to work in this area.

The climate for venture capitalism is being affected by the 1986 tax law which eliminates the capital gains tax rate. Lowering the regular tax rate and eliminating the capital gains tax rate should hurt venture capitalism. According to James Blair, some people argue that if you lower the rates it doesn't make any difference, but a meaningful differential must be maintained in order to get people to commit their funds for a long period of time as opposed to a short period of time. While that doesn't directly hurt the flow of funds of the venture capital, it does indirectly because the ability to become liquid is really through the sale of entities in the public market.

Another factor to consider is the availability of money for venture capital. As the economy strengthens, more money is available for investment and there is enough excess money so that people are willing to take risks with their money. Expect to see more venture capital money available in the next few years for university-based deals and new startups.

The money will go where the technology lies hidden; venture capitalists don't care where the technology is as long as it is accessible for product development. If the venture capitalists control the company, the odds are good that they will try to sell the startup to another company or on the public market. In biotechnology that was the case for Hybritech. Formed by Kleiner Perkins Caufield, the venture capitalists hired the president and everybody else and built the business until they sold it to Eli Lilly. The venture capitalist has to plan for when he can liquidate his investment; otherwise, he's out of business.

In summary, there are several methods of financing the entrepreneurial company that tie it into both the university for the research and the large corporation for the revenue-bearing contracts. The traditional venture capital route has changed with biotechnology, where for the first time venture capital was invested in companies whose products were years away from completion. Entrepreneurial companies used this money to assemble a company that was large enough to align itself with universities, perform research for corporations and keep a bit of its proprietary research for itself. The contracts with major corporations led to more contracts and then to public stock market financing, each form of financing building upon the last. One recent development is the existence of venture capital pools that make use of the RDLP structure, making the small investor a "mini" venture capitalist. As we shall see in Chapter 9, the RDLP is a complicated form of financing whose popularity is threatened by the recent tax reform measures.

9 The Research and Development Limited Partnership: Potentials and Problems

Research and development limited partnership (RDLPs) contribute in numerous ways to the spread of entrepreneurial science. This form of financing offers unique advantages to small- and medium-sized entrepreneurial firms as well as investors, large corporations and universities.

There are several forms that RDLPs can take. The general partner usually consists of a group of people who also manage the corporation that started the RDLP. The general partner can also be the management of an investment house, as in the case of the blind pool RDLPs that invest their money in a range of companies. The limited partner is always the investor; he has no say in the management of the partnership, which is entrusted to the general partner. The limited partner could be an entrepreneur, the small investor reached through the blind pools, or a group of corporations interested in conducting joint research, as is the case with the Software Productivity Consortium. The research can be performed by a branch of the company that formed the partnership, another company, or a university or non-profit research institution. These are the main forms that the RDLP can take.

A study recently conducted by Lois Peters and Herbert Fusfeld of the NYU Center for Science and Technology policy estimates the impact these financial vehicles are having.[1] According to their database, between 1978–1985 there were $2.5 billion in RDLP offerings. These are growing at a rate of about $.5 billion per year, thanks in large part to the formation of blind pools that bring venture capital financing to the investor of moderate means. About 95 percent of the investments were made with small firms contributing the technology. The database shows a similar number of transactions for computers (thirty-five), electronics (thirty-eight) and biotechnology (thirty-five). Ranked by total amount of money raised, the top firms were, first, biotechnology, then computers, medical technology and electronics. The total number of expenditures accounts for .5 percent of all U.S. R&D expenditures and 1 percent of corporate R&D expenditures. The researchers estimate that RDLPs provided 31 percent of the $1.6 billion that small companies spent on R&D in 1983. This means that even though RDLPs only represent a tiny portion of total U.S. R&D, they play a very large role in what is the most innovative sector of the economy.

Who should take advantage of research and development limited partnerships in their businesses? When is it advantageous for universities, venture capitalists, or research consortiums to participate? The advantages for the private corporation clearly exist as long as the company obeys certain rules to overcome potential objections by the Internal Revenue Service. When one company controls the general partner, the company can raise money through limited partnerships without diluting its equity or creating a debt. This is known as "off balance sheet" financing. Another advantage for the company is retention of control over the research, since the limited partners have no say in management of the research. This situation contrasts with the use of equity financing or venture capital where stockholders have a voice in management. The stock offering dilutes the original ownership of the company to a greater extent than the RDLP. Another advantage for the corporation to use RDLP financing is availability of second-round financing; the RDLP allows a company to become involved in second-round financing of the newly developed technology without incurring substantial risks for the initial research and development. The RDLP allows the company to take risks in a new format; it is another alternative for financing R&D. The limited partner bears most of the monetary risk in the RDLP; the company loses little if the research fails, although it has an opportunity cost. The RDLP therefore encourages participating companies to fund risky R&D which it might not otherwise fund because of its inability to incur debt or its unwillingness due to the high cost of capital. The RDLP opens up the area of corporate research that is nonessential but potentially profitable. This is the niche for the RDLP. Finally, the company can buy out the technology from the partnership by exercising a buy-out option in the agreement. This allows the company, when it is advantageous, to buy out the royalty rights with cash or equity; this can be a good deal for both the company and the limited partner.

For the investor in RDLPs, the small company is the appropriate investment target. The investment should have a high potential of return in two to three years. A small company will grow from the results; in contrast, research financed for a large company may be a diversion from the company's main business. The investor has an additional advantage when aiming for the small company. He can usually get better terms because the funding is more critical for small firms than for large firms.

The large corporation is not usually recommended as a target for the RDLP. However, under certain circumstances the RDLP may be beneficial. For example, if the company is very competitive but is not large enough to match the R&D resources of its competitors, an RDLP might be recommended. In another case, it may need to diversify and will choose the RDLP for technical enhancement. A technical program may, if successful, require some form of joint venture for manufacturing or marketing. In this instance, the RDLP can share the risks of the project. Finally, a company with financial limitations may need this form of financing because it is off the balance sheet, i.e., not reported as debt.

A major disadvantage for large companies to engage in RDLP's is the fact that the projects may detract from the main business of the corporation, causing a strain on the corporate in-house research staff or requiring the hiring of inexperienced researchers. The RDLP might distract the company from its main line of business, affecting the motivations and planning of technical R&D managers. If the project is a winner, the corporation tends to lose its focus. If the project is not in the main line of the company's business, it has greater uncertainty attached to it. Misapplication of the research could lead to major corporate disappointment in a company that is not accustomed to spending research money in this way. RDLPs constitute ''impatient money,'' usually requiring results in two to three years. Major corporations would usually prefer to go for more patient money. Large companies may also find that they have access to money loaned at more favorable terms than the payback of the RDLP.

Despite these disadvantages, Becton Dickinson decided to launch an RDLP, as analyzed by Fusfeld and Peters in their book, *Research and Development Limited Partnerships and Their Significance for In-*

novation. The company needed to keep its balance sheet attractive in order to fight takeover attempts by Sun Oil Co. Sales were not rising and profits were down. Becton Dickinson had to rely upon its considerable research strengths to pull through. It could borrow the money, but interest rates in 1981 were prohibitive. The least expensive way for Becton Dickinson to conduct the research which it needed to do to remain competitive was to finance it through an RDLP. It hired Paine Webber Development Corporation to structure one, making an offering of $43.7 million in September 1983. This enabled the company to conduct research in immunodiagnostics, microbiology and cellular analysis. Two products are already on the market, three are in development, and one product has been dropped. Modest royalty checks have been sent to investors. It turned out that if all projects had been successful, Becton Dickinson would have effectively borrowed the money at a 20 percent rate. Becton Dickinson is expected to do another RDLP in the near future.

RDLPs have been conducted with universities with varying degrees of success. The University of California, for example, has participated in twenty of these ventures. The nature of the university is not conducive to research that should have results in two to three years. Therefore, using the university as the research contractor can lead the investors to disappointment in the university for the wrong reasons. It can also cause problems on campus; the direct exposure of entrepreneurial money without an organization to back it up can pose problems for researchers. Finally, some universities may want to limit interactions to the point where financiers are discouraged from investing in the research.

The Department of Commerce's Bruce Merrifield feels that the research and development limited partnership should play a crucial role in financing both companies and research cooperatives. He is most concerned about transforming entire industries by pooling research. Claims Merrifield, "No individual company can risk and bet its whole company on next generation high-risk technology, but a consortium can do this, sharing the risk, pooling resources, collapsing the development time—and this is our only hope in terms of recapturing technical industrial leadership." The R&D limited partnership, a thirty-year-old tax law, is one means of supporting this entrepreneurial science.

Let's examine some RDLPs to see how they work. Genentech has successfully initiated three RDLPs. The first, Genentech Clinical Partners (GCP), was started in 1982 to examine therapeutic use of human growth hormone and gamma interferon. The program tested the use of recombinant human growth hormone for hypopituitary dwarfism, constitutionally delayed short stature, and cachexia. It also performed preclinical and clinical testing of recombinant gamma interferon with respect to a variety of cancers and viral diseases. Finally, the program examined alternative delivery systems for these preparations, including oral, topical and implantable dosages in addition to injectable forms of administration. It raised $55 million and paid its first royalties to investors in early 1986 from the sale of human growth hormone. The second RDLP, initiated in 1983, tested Tissue-type Plasminogen Activator (TPA) under Genentech Clinical Partners II (GCP II). $33.9 million was raised under GCP II, with expectations of returns to investors starting in early 1987 with the marketing of a TPA product. Finally, in 1984 and January of 1985 Genentech launched Genentech Clinical Partners III (GCP III) to test the anti-cancer properties of Tumor Necrosis Factor. GCP III yielded $33 million. Paine Webber and Hambrecht & Quist marketed GCP; Paine Webber alone sold GCP II and GCP III.

Why did Genentech choose the RDLP structure? It wanted to become a fully integrated research, manufacturing and marketing company in the pharmaceuticals business and it saw that the RDLP could help them achieve that goal. Genentech's previous track record was tremendous. It turned a profit for seven years straight while growing explosively. Clinical trials are extremely expensive. Genentech wanted to take the money for the testing as revenue and not report the clinical testing as a loss on its balance sheet. It also wanted to keep its debt-to-equity ratio low. By refining the limited partnership concept it was able to accomplish all of this. Thomas Kiley, vice president for corporate development, is critical of companies that started RDLPs without the proper product focus. By focusing on products, Genentech knew exactly what it owned and what could be predicted as the investor's return. Genentech recently bought out investors in GCP and GCP II to gain favorable tax and accounting treatment. It paid out 3,000 shares of stock worth about $240,000 for each $50,000 limited partnership investment in GCP. For GCP II it paid out 2,500 shares worth about $200,000 for every $50,000 investment.

In order for the limited partner to receive capital gains treatment under the old tax laws, there had to be a continuing business for a specified period of time to satisfy holding requirements. Genentech therefore set up a joint venture with the limited partners. Genentech retains the option to buy back all of the technology from the limited partners, an option it logically exercised with the first two partnerships. Once the option is chosen, the joint venture dissolves. Having the option in the contract keeps the limited partners at risk. The limited partners also benefited from the R&D tax credit; although all three RDLPs are for clinical testing, the IRS considers this to be research despite the fact that there is a great deal of knowledge about the development of the product. The royalties depend upon how much product you sell, but the standard that investment bankers consider in this situation yields a 35 percent annual return on investment.

Kiley is not concerned about whether the 1986 tax law will affect future RDLPs that Genentech might contemplate. He explains that this type of RDLP is driven much more by equity features than by the tax shelter features that would become less significant since the maximum income tax has been lowered. These RDLPs are more aptly described as tax-advantaged ventures because the tax consequences pale by comparison to the equity return. Especially given Genentech's success with the previous three RDLPs, it would not be deterred by the tax law changes from starting additional ones.

Centocor is another example of a company which relied upon its RDLP to fund its product development. Centocor Oncogene Research Partners, L. P. (CORP) was established to develop products for the monitoring and diagnosis of specific cancers through the use of knowledge of oncogenes, genes that play a role in initiating the cancer process. CORP has contracts with Centocor, Inc. as well as universities and non-profit foundations for research into cancer with emphasis upon Human T-Cell Leukemia Virus, the virus that causes AIDS. Arrangements were made with the Dana Farber Cancer Institute for work on breast, lung, and ovarian cancer research; Duke University for research on ovarian cancer; Massachusetts General Hospital, for work on liver cancer; and Max-Planck-Institut Fur Molekulare Genetik on the generation of proteins and antigens associated with specific oncogenes.

The deal, originally structured for $20 million, was modified due to depressed market conditions to $5 million according to Michael Dura of L. F. Rothschild, who structured the transactions. It closed in August of 1984. $40,000 units were sold with each unit containing 2,500 warrants exercisable at $12 per share. Centocor complicated the deal by loaning money to the partnership. The fixed buyout option was for 4,400 shares of stock or $184,000 in cash less repayment of any outstanding balance. Centocor came to Rothschild in 1986 to inform them that the underlying technology would not meet the development schedule that was contemplated. Centocor was not interested in buying out the partnership, but they wanted to purchase the technology. They bought out the technology in February of 1986, paying back the investor $26,000 in cash and forgiving the third installment payments of the loan, resulting in an after-tax internal rate of return of 22 percent exclusive of the value of the warrants. At the time the stock was trading at $32 per share, so the intrinsic value of the warrants was $50,000. Adding together the value of the warrants and the cash, the investor received the equivalent of $76,000 for a $23,000 investment.

Rothschild recently structured another deal with a biotechnology company called Xoma. The units went for $50,000 each payable over three years. There was a fixed buyout option for either 2,200 shares of common stock or $112,500. The after-tax internal rate of return was 33 percent with the cash option and more than this with the stock option. The company approached Rothschild in December of 1985 with the prospect of going public. Xoma determined that they needed additional funds and that the initial public offering was the best method of financing. Unfortunately, most of the company's technology was tied up in the limited partnership. They needed to buy this back so that they would control the technology. They did not have the cash position to buy out the partners; furthermore, the stock was not yet publicly traded and the options were less than attractive. In May of 1986 Xoma offered to change each limited partnership unit into a $100,000 principal amount convertible debenture at 6.25 percent, convertible into the underlying common stock at the initial offering price. The initial offering took place a week later at $16 per share. The after-tax rate of return was 47 percent. The Contocor and Xoma deals indicate that even if all does not go as well as expected, the limited partner can gain a great deal through the RDLP.

One trend in RDLPs worth noting is the rise in pooled funds, where investment companies collect funding from wealthy individuals and institutions and manage the distribution of money to high-technology startups. The small investor can, with these vehicles, provide venture capital money for the first time. He or she benefits from the advantage of good money management skills by the investment firm, allowing the risk to be spread over a number of different investments. Some of the firms involved in pooled RDLPs include E. F. Hutton, Merrill Lynch, Morgan Stanley Ventures, Paine Webber, Prudential Bache, and Hambrecht & Quist. These funds usually require that the investor have substantial means. For example, Merrill Lynch requires that the investor have $100,000 net worth and a gross income of $50,000 or more for the first four years of investment. The investment minimums vary. Laidlow Technology Venture Partners may be the lowest, with a minimum of $2,500. Other funds examined range from $3,000 to $5,000 as a minimum. Pools are also open to institutional money for corporations choosing to invest in high technology. Peters and Fusfeld estimate that from 1978 to 1985 over $574 million was raised by the pooled funds.

The pooled funds and any other RDLP arrangement suffer if the IRS disallows the RDLP, treating it as a corporation, according to analysis provided by the Department of Commerce. Four criteria have been established by Treasury regulations to be used in weighing whether a partnership is considered a corporation: continuity of life, centralization of management, limited liability for members of the partnership, and free transferability of partnership interests. If more than two of the criteria mentioned here are met, then the partnership is treated as a corporation for tax purposes.

Let's take a look at these criteria in more detail. The partnership has continuity of life, according to the Treasury, "if the death, insanity, bankruptcy, retirement, resignation, or expulsion of any member will not cause a dissolution of the agreement." It is possible to structure RDLP's so that the death, retirement, or insanity of a general partner does dissolve the partnership.

The issue of centralization of management is a more difficult standard to overcome. The Treasury is not specific about what constitutes centralization, which it defines as "substantial" ownership by the limited partners. However, it gives examples where the general partnership owns between 6 and 20 percent for avoiding centralization of management.

When do the individual partners have limited liability? Treasury regulations state that the limited partnership will have this corporate identifier if the general partner "has no substantial assets (other than his interest in the partnership) which could be reached by a creditor of the organization and when he is merely a 'dummy' acting as the agent of the limited partners.'' The IRS has revealed its criteria in several rulings: in summary, the general partner must have a net worth of 10 percent of the total contributions to the partnership, if the general partner has an interest in only one limited partnership and if total contributions are at least $2.5 million. The partnership will otherwise be treated as a corporation. An IRS revenue procedure states that the general partner must own at least one percent of the partnership. An additional criteria for partnership status requires that the total of tax deductions from the partnership be no greater than the amount of equity capital invested in the limited partnership.

For the criteria of free transferability of partnership interests, the IRS has defined this corporate characteristic as the power of each of its members to substitute for themselves, in the same organization and without the consent of others, a person who is not a member of the organization.

In addition to structuring the RDLP to avoid IRS problems, the entrepreneurs involved in RDLPs must consider antitrust implications. This is particularly true for corporations from the same industry who join together to perform R&D. The courts are working on a "rule of reason" type of analysis that takes into consideration the various procompetitive benefits of joint R&D. When several companies join together in RDLPs, they are likely to be ruled in violation of antitrust laws only if the collaboration is likely, on balance, to be anti-competitive in light of the surrounding circumstances. These companies would violate the law if a joint R&D venture served as a device though which participants could coordinate prices and output on current production in a market where they will compete. In this unlikely event, the collaboration would be acting as a merger. Some factors to consider are: extent to which current prices, cost or output is exchanged among members; concentration of the participants in the relevant markets; the market share of the joint venture; and the nature of the R&D and the goods and services produced by each participant.

Another antitrust implication occurs when the partnership includes too large a fraction of firms capable of undertaking the same or similar R&D. In this event, the desire to succeed or to risk failure is reduced because of lack of competition in the marketplace. RDLPs structured as joint ventures should have the opposite effect, increasing the level and efficiency of competition. According to one Department of Commerce document, "so long as there is a sufficient number of firms participating in competing R&D so that a significant number (perhaps five) of other projects can be formed to do competitive R&D on a scale similar to that of the joint venture, then the potential adverse effect of the incentives to innovate will be so small as not to be of a concern under antitrust laws."

Another antitrust concern is the case where participating companies in a joint RDLP venture have restrictions of one form or another that aren't directly related to the conduct of R&D. The courts will look at the nature of these restrictions and the degree to which they are unrelated to the R&D as well as the overall competitive effects of the venture.

There are two types of reward structures for the investor as limited partner. In the royalty partnership, he gets royalties on sales of the products of the technology. Many royalty RDLPs have equity kickers; the limited partner gets equity in the sponsoring company instead of a new spin-off.

In the equity partnership, in contrast to the royalty partnership, the limited partner gets equity in a new corporation in lieu of royalties. In either case, there is a holding period for the technology in order to treat it as an asset instead of inventory. This is usually a period of twelve months from the time the technology is reduced to practice. The technology is usually licensed to the participating company with an option to purchase it after twelve months.

Some promoters give the impression that the RDLP is "free money" for the corporation because the company loses nothing if the research fails. It turns out, however, that if you compare it with debt financing, it can be very expensive if the project succeeds. Peters and Fusfeld analyze Agrigenetics Research Associates Limited, a $55 million RDLP funded in 1981 that has projected an after-tax yield of 50.95 percent per year for 1981–1991, assuming a 50 percent tax bracket. Although this is expensive, it is the option to choose if the company can't raise debt financing or doesn't want to dilute its equity. The money can best be considered as a particular form of venture capital. It's an alternative to the traditional forms of venture capital when people want to test a research idea. It can spread the risk of R&D when each project is part of a portfolio. Finally, for pooled RDLPs, the financial management houses become managers of R&D, improving the probabilities of profit from successful R&D. They also avoid the conflict of interest inherent when the sponsoring company is also the general partner; in this case, the company has to choose the appropriate field for research with an eye toward improving the total profitability of the company, even if it is at the expense of the limited partner.

How do RDLPs contribute to the innovation process and the overall economy? First of all, they broaden the spectrum of research options to meet the timing needs of innovation. They do not inspire new research ideas so much as they exploit existing research ideas that would not otherwise be tested. RDLPs support small high-tech companies that play an important role in the overall innovation of the economy. It is often mentioned that countries like Japan have the financial strength in their large companies to make the best use of their R&D ideas. They have a cost of capital advantage over U.S. firms. America's counteracting influence is the small, high-tech firm. The RDLP corrects for underinvestment in useful R&D. It also broadens the spectrum of financing options, allowing for greater flexibility in the economy. For these reasons, tax policy should be formulated that protects the RDLP and encourages its use.

In summary, the RDLP is an attractive alternative to other forms of corporate financing, particularly for a company that wants to raise money with less dilution of equity, and without going deeper into debt or affecting the balance sheet. It supports high-risk ideas for testing with an affordable payback, often in royalties of 7 to 10 percent of product sales. It is more expensive than debt financing, but the RDLP takes more of the risk away from the sponsoring company. This tool for entrepreneurial science is threatened by the 1986 tax law changes, although the RDLP will probably survive for institutional investors interested in supporting R&D through blind pools. The RDLP should be encouraged, particularly for joint research projects within industries, because it allows procompetitive research to be funded in such a way that the overall level of technology in the United States will be increased in comparison to the Japanese and other competitors. It will improve the efficiency of product development for entire industries. The RDLP can also be seen as an innovation enhancer that provides an additional type of option for the corporate investor. The RDLP should be encouraged for the sake of entrepreneurial science and the U.S. economy.

10   Government Strategies in R&D: A Comparison

Throughout the course of research for this book American business-men have told of their concerns for domination of markets by the Japanese and, to a lesser extent, Europeans. These executives, particularly in the microelectronics and related industries, have marvelled at Japanese progress and expressed concern about current attempts in the United States to maintain or develop the best markets for their goods. A comparison of the efforts in the United States with controlled, co-ordinated efforts by the governments of Japan, West Germany, France and the United Kingdom reveals that there is some cause for alarm. However, the U.S. government's strategy of non-intervention in cor-porate affairs may work well if pro-competitive research strategies grow. It is instructive to look first at overall R&D funding in these countries and then examine funding in microelectronics and biotechnology on a country-by-country basis.

A report by the National Science Foundation comparing all types of sponsored R&D as a function of gross national product shows that the United States is ahead of all other countries.[1] In 1981, the last year in which figures were tallied for all countries, the United States spent $72.1 billion on R&D from government, industrial and university re-sources. This is greater than the combined R&D of France, West Ger-many, Japan, and the United Kingdom. According to government sources, in 1983 the United States spent about $7.7 billion on com-puters, semiconductors and related equipment while Japanese industry spent approximately $2.2 billion.

These figures can be deceptive. For example, a significant portion of the United States spending on microelectronics R&D entailed military applications, which don't translate easily into non-military products. In fact, according to a recent General Accounting Office (GAO) report the U.S. government is spending less on efforts to develop nondefense microelectronics than any of the four countries.[2] The U.S. effort was reported to be about $80 million versus spending by each of the other countries in excess of $100 million.

Since military R&D does not necessarily translate into products for private industry, it is helpful to compare the non-military R&D for each country. A report from the NSF shows that since 1970, West Germany and Japan have had a higher percentage of their gross national product devoted to nonmilitary R&D than the United States.[3] However, the United States still outspends all countries being compared. In contrast to popular perceptions of the extent of Japanese government funding for R&D, figures from an NSF report show that in 1983 industry funded 64 percent of total R&D there compared with 50 percent in the United States; the rest of the funding is supplied by the governments or universities.

The total work force available for technology is one additional measure of the potential for entrepreneurial science. Japan graduates more engineers than the United States or European countries. The National Science Foundation is trying to correct this by encouraging engineering students on U.S. campuses. The United States graduates more natural scientists than Japan and employs the largest number of scientists in R&D programs. An NSF report also shows that the United States produces a larger number of doctoral graduates in the natural sciences and engineering than Japan or West Germany.[4] These figures indicate that the supply of scientists for entrepreneurial science should be adequate in the United States when compared with the competition.

There are some ominous signs in the statistics, however. Eric Bloch, the head of the National Science Foundation, recently wrote in an issue of *Science* that smaller numbers of bright students are being attracted to the sciences in the United States.[5] Equally disturbing is the fact that the number of U.S. students earning Ph.D.s in the sciences is down from the 1970's figures. As a measure of our country's scientific output, he claims that the U.S. share of scientific and technical literature declined between 1973 and 1982. Mathematics dropped by 23 percent, physics dropped by 18 percent, and biology dropped by 17 percent. The U.S. scientific literature is also decreasing in citation ratios, the extent to which U.S. literature is cited in proportion to its volume. This means that other countries are catching up to us.

Bloch believes that we must strengthen our universities and make the sciences more attractive for graduate studies. Since the United States tends to lose candidates for graduate studies to industry, the NSF should provide more grants for students and lobby for better salaries for science professors.

The basic issue facing the U.S. government now is whether its noninterventionist stance will prevail when the other governments are actively bringing companies together, paying for research expenses, and encouraging collaboration among competitors. It is our view that the U.S. government should provide badly needed targets for industry. A look at the international competition supports this view.

Japan holds the record for long-term governmental planning in microelectronics. In 1981 it announced a twelve-year, $500 million program called Basic Technology for Electronic Computers, known better as the Fifth Generation computer project. The project aims to use very large scale integrated circuits to apply artificial intelligence research, manufacturing computers that can translate language, create computer software automatically and serve as interactive reference libraries. It was this project that stimulated the formation of the Microelectronics and Computer Technology Consortium and the Semiconductor Research Corporation in the United States.

Japanese R&D funding in microelectronics comes from three main sources, the Science and Technology Agency (STA), the Ministry of International Trade and Industry (MITI), and the Ministry of Education (ME). MITI is known to collaborate with groups of companies to perform research with a budget of about $50 million per year. It established a non-profit foundation and linked eight companies together for the Fifth Generation computer project. Another example is MITI's cosponsorship of a project with six companies to develop a high-speed computer for scientific purposes; the project is scheduled to last from 1981–1989.

The Japanese government established another program in 1981 that includes advanced work in biotechnology and microelectronics over the course of ten years. Ten companies are working together in the microelectronics component of the program under a group called the Research and Development Association for Future Electronic Devices.

MITI organized this group and funded additional research in its Elec-tro-Technical Laboratories with an annual budget of about $40 million in 1982.

In biotechnology, the STA, MITI, and the Ministry of Agriculture, Forestry, and Fisheries (MAFF) have specifically targeted R&D in Ja-pan, according to a report issued by the U.S. Congressional Office of Technology Assessment (OTA). MITI started a ten-year program in 1981 in bioreactors, recombinant DNA technology and mass cell cul-ture to diffuse biotechnology into the private sector. Fourteen compa-nies participate with MITI in the projects, funded at $103 million. Most of the work is conducted in industrial laboratories, all paid for by MITI. The STA is funding generic research programs of similar dimensions as MITI's program. Finally, the MAFF is spending a com-parable amount for R&D performed for industry in its laboratories and is funding research taking place in industrial labs. Three other govern-ment agencies are funding basic and applied research in biotechnol-ogy. The OTA estimates that the total funding for Japanese biotech R&D was $67 million in 1983, far less than the U.S. government's programs. The major difference is that a preponderance of U.S. fund-ing is for basic research, while Japan's funding is oriented more toward applied research.

As long as Japan takes advantage of freely published research at American universities, it does not need to bolster its basic research component. In a sense, the United States is doing the basic research for the Japanese while Japan concentrates on actual product develop-ment.

In fiscal year 1985, the Japanese government spent an estimated $247 million on biotechnology research, regulation and administra-tion, according to the Japan Economic Institute. Leading the list in terms of spending is the Ministry of Education with $100 million, most of which flows into universities and national research institutes. ME is underwriting over eighty gene bank projects. The Ministry of Health and Welfare had budgeted $60 million in 1985 for biotechnol-ogy. The bulk of these funds supports the complicated drug testing and approval system. The ministry also funds some modest industry cooperative projects using alpha interferon and interleukin-2 for cancer treatment evaluation.

The Ministry of Agriculture, Forestry and Fisheries budgeted $50 million for biotechnology in 1985. MAFF is trying to develop a cell fusion process to produce fertile hybrid plants in cooperation with Kikkoman Corp. A group of fourteen companies is exploring other cell fusion techniques with MAFF footing most of the projected $150 million cost of the eight-year project. The Ministry of International Trade and Industry has allocated $21 million in its budget for biotechnology; a large part of this funds research with industry on commercial applications of biotechnology. MITI also recently established the Japan Key Technology Center, which joined forces with five Japanese companies to develop modified natural proteins for use in bioelectronics. MITI also wants to spend $40 million over the coming decade to develop an organic computer modelled after the human brain. MITI's Electrochemical Laboratory has begun working with NEC Corp. on bioelectronic circuits, the first step toward an analog computer. Meanwhile, MITI is completing a seven-year, $149 million program on the production and use of biomass.

Despite all of these programs, one scholar of Japanese biotechnology and a contractor for the OTA report on biotechnology's commercialization, Gary Saxonhouse, believes that Japanese government influence on biotechnology is small. He concludes that "examination of the familiar instruments of industrial policy indicates that Japan gives less formal aid and comfort to its high technology sectors and to biotechnology in particular than do the governments of most other advanced industrialized countries." He considers other factors such as tariffs, development of capital markets through government influence, and government-industry cooperative research programs as well as outlays for government-sponsored R&D.

There are indeed many factors to consider when evaluating Japanese performance in biotechnology. In the private sector American firms (excluding drug companies) outspent Japanese R&D ten to one ($500 to $700 million versus $50 to $70 million) according to figures compiled by the Japan Economic Institute. Mark Dibner of DuPont writes in *Science* that the Japanese government in 1984 spent only $50 to $60 million for biotechnology research related to pharmaceuticals, about one-tenth of that spent by the United States.[6] More than half of the Japanese funding went for applied research. A lack of a broad base in fundamental research and a lack of venture capital in Japan make it more difficult for the Japanese to catch up with U.S. R&D. Furthermore, the funding for R&D by private industry is small compared with the United States. In 1985 the four largest established American companies in biotechnology spent $468 million, which is 15 percent more than the entire Japanese biotech R&D expenditure.[7] In the same *Nihon Keizai Shinbun* survey, it was shown that the four largest newly established American biotechnology firms spent more than twice what the four most active established Japanese companies spent on R&D. The information sharing that takes place when the Japanese government brings together corporations makes up for a smaller amount of information sharing taking place between corporate scientists when compared with those in the United States, who are raised in the university tradition and attend more conferences than the Japanese scientists.

The OTA gave a fairly optimistic view of America's continued lead in biotechnology while it warned that Japanese government planning will help Japan provide stiff competition. Other experts are more pessimistic. Gene Gregory, a professor of business at Tokyo's Sophia University, sees parallels in biotechnology with the development of the microelectronics industry in the late sixties and warns that the Japanese might win a significant share of the world's markets once again. He sees the acute shortage of personnel combined with the high cost of capital and instability within venture capital companies as factors restricting the high level of innovation required for the United States to maintain its lead. He concludes that in the United States, the much weaker generation of new biotechnology firms is now confronted with the same prospect of shortages of staff and money. Both assets are more readily available to established and more highly integrated Japanese firms with long experience in bioprocess engineering on which to build future growth. Unless these gaps are filled, a repetition of the patterns of change in the electronics industry would seem a foregone conclusion to him.

We differ with Gregory, seeing that the environments of the two technologies are complex. Venture companies are not as unstable as Gregory believes, thanks to a fresh infusion of funding by Wall Street in 1986. The venture companies that are unstable will lead to incorporation of these companies into larger multinational firms situated in the United States. These acquisitions should lead to greater economies of scale such as the ones enjoyed by large Japanese pharmaceutical and food firms.

The race in biotechnology between Japan and the United States is most evident in the area of basic research. According to Ronald Cape, Chairman of Cetus Corporation, the United States has enjoyed its lead in biotechnology precisely because of generous government funding of research in the past. The Japanese, in their catch-up strategy, have failed so far to duplicate the American university system and the federal support for research there. Unfortunately, research funding levels in the United States have plateaued or, in some cases, dropped. Cape argues that we must excel in what we do best, the basic research, if biotechnology is not to suffer the fate of automobiles, steel, VCRs and electronic chips. He is certain that the Japanese can eventually revamp their university system to catch up. Furthermore, they are more aware of the international race in biotechnology than we are. At one point Cape argued for a National Biotechnology Agency that would help ensure that basic research became an even more important priority.

Cape believes that the free enterprise system has worked well in the development of biotechnology. He does not advocate a government targeting system for the United States, nor does he claim that the government should do a great deal of applied research. Industry has already shown that it can successfully conduct the applied research. Cape believes it to be important to let the current system work, the system which has so far maintained leadership in biotechnology.

The United Kingdom intends to be competitive in both microelectronics and biotechnology against the United States with the help of a range of government-sponsored programs. It embarked in 1983 on a five-year, $300 million plan called the Program for Advanced Information Technology (the Alvey Program). The Alvey Program involves working on large scale integrated circuits, computer programming, better interaction between people and computers, and systems that can apply knowledge through inference. The program, managed through the Department of Trade and Industry (DTI), spends about $72 million on university research and about $216 million on industrial research with matching funds provided by industry. Support for the Alvey program is shared by DTI, the Ministry of Defense (MD) and the Department of Education and Science (DES). The DES regulates university research and the DTI manages government laboratories and supports R&D in private industry. The DTI engages in cooperative research projects with groups of companies; in addition, it provides capital for investment in new companies and supplies loans for promising projects. The DE's Science and Engineering Research Council spent about $13 million in 1983 for information engineering. The MD, in contrast, spent about $412 million in 1983 on military-related electronics technology.

In biotechnology, the British government started two companies, Agricultural Genetics Co. and Celltech, to commercialize biotechnology, and in 1982 established a three-year, $30 million program for industrial biotechnology. This program funds consultancies, pays for project feasibility studies, and sponsors joint industry-research centers. The government has also established a Biotechnology Directorate at the Science and Engineering Research Council (SERC) to coordinate all government-sponsored biotech R&D. The United Kingdom funds generic applied research at several locations and works to create interdisciplinary programs at universities throughout the country. The OTA estimates that the British government spent between $56 and $60 million on all phases of biotech R&D in 1982, roughly the equivalent of spending levels in France, West Germany, and Japan. Expect that the British will be a major competitor with the United States in specific product markets in biotechnology. They have the critical mass of personnel with outstanding university research. Government coordination is making up for the past lack of university-industry cooperation.

The Federal Republic of Germany should be examined because it will be a major competitor against the United States in both microelectronics and biotechnology. It has quietly entered the microelectronics race on a government planning level. In a program launched in 1983, it is spending about $1.1 billion total dollars on the Microelectronics Research Program. Areas included in the program are microelectronics, advanced computers, office automation, communications and robotics. West Germany's main funding establishment for R&D is the Ministry of Research and Technology, which receives about 58 percent of the government's R&D funds and spends about half of its budget for research projects in industry. It supports several independent research organizations and thirteen national research centers.

West Germany coordinates its strategy in biotechnology through the Federal Ministry for Research and Technology (BMFT, Bundesministerium fur Forschung und Technologie). BMFT supports biotech through funding set aside for R&D, grants to industry, and shared coordination of funding with other government agencies. For the biotechnology program BMFT spent $29 million in 1982. The OTA estimates contributions of $20 to $40 million to the Max Planck Society and the German Research Society for a total expenditure of between $49 and $69 million.[8] The government also supports the privately funded Society for Biotechnological Research, which conducts generic bioprocessing research for industry. The government has encouraged coordinated research programs between some of the country's largest pharmaceutical companies and its research universities.

Expect West Germany to be a stiff competitor in the bioengineering side of biotechnology, but don't expect a smooth flow of research results from the university laboratory to industry. The German university system, compared with that in the United States, is inflexible about its relations with industry.

The United Kingdom, France and West Germany have also banded together in a European consortium aimed at competing with the United States and Japan in microelectronics. Called the European Stragetic Program of Research and Development in Information Technology (ESPRIT), the program will last five years and cost the participating governments about $640 million. Industrial corporations participating in the program are expected to pay an equal amount. Designed for Europe to compete with Japan and the United States, ESPRIT is organized around five themes: development of large scale integrated circuits; improvements in the theoretical foundation of software technology and in practical applications; the development of advanced information processing techniques; the development of office automation technology; and computer-integrated manufacturing systems that will integrate design, manufacturing, engineering, test, repair and assembly by using a common data-base. ESPRIT was planned to complement the activity by individual countries. It therefore participates on long-term, non-military research involving research cooperation between companies, research institutes or universities in at least two countries.

The U.S. government, in contrast, is spending $600 million over five years in microelectronics research with emphasis upon military applications. Begun in 1983, the Strategic Computing Program (SCP) aims at both national security and economic growth. Its goals include applications in artificial intelligence, very large scale integrated systems, high performance device systems, and computer architecture. The program is under the management of the Department of Defense's Defense Advanced Research Projects Agency (DARPA). Research is conducted both in universities and in government laboratories. In addition, the armed forces are major investors in microelectronics R&D, contributing $149.6 million in research in 1984.

The National Science Foundation (NSF) also supports electronics research at universities. In 1984 it provided about $45 million for related research at universities and spent an additional $35 million for training researchers and developing fundamental knowledge for computer systems. Additional funding for computer electronics includes projects coordinated by the National Bureau of Standards and the National Aeronautics and Space Administration.

To the degree that spending levels translate into commitment to product development, the United States is far ahead of its competition. The U.S. government spent $511 million annually for basic research in biotechnology when figures from 1982 and 1983 were compiled by the OTA.[9] This figure is higher than the combined expenditures of Japan, the United Kingdom, France and West Germany. U.S. government expenditures for applied generic research are only $6.4 million, although this amount might range as high as $20 to $30 million if totals from the U.S. Department of Agriculture and the Department of Energy were added to the total. This figure lags well behind spending totals for generic applied research by the United Kingdom, West Germany, and the world's leader, Japan. Given the ease with which Japan can learn from our open system of university research and their superior applied research capability, the United States has reason to assume that Japanese competition will be fierce. The United States does not have an industrial policy to counter this competition.

Apart from spending large amounts of money to fund research, each of the governments aids R&D through tax provisions. The United States differs in supporting programs for small business development. The West German and French governments focus on loan subsidies and guarantees because the business climate in these two countries requires that companies borrow rather than sell stock. In Japan the government actually finances the companies in a way that invites private lenders to work with the firms.

The United States can do more to encourage entrepreneurial science without resorting to collaboration with industry. First of all, it is important to acknowledge that the figures for U.S. R&D investment in biotechnology and microelectronics indicate that a high degree of participation by government already exists. The relatively low proportion of generic applied research is being accommodated to some extent by the NSF's new engineering research centers. Although the record shows that the United States has slipped by many standards, it still has the unqualified lead in total R&D, biotechnology, and some aspects of microelectronics. The United States is right to worry about Japan as a competitor. That country by one estimate has recently proven to be six times as efficient as the United States in developing and marketing pharmaceutical products. Japan can also capitalize on the U.S. research base in biotechnology. In addition to taking advantage of university research, a number of Japanese companies have invested in biotech startups to get a window on the technology.

The United States can and should do more to encourage entrepreneurial science through additional tax incentives for engineering research. The NSF should continue moving in the direction of being a helper and shaper for applied research. It should be able to give more grants to interdisciplinary research, particularly in the bioengineering areas of biotechnology. It should also increase its support for university-industry cooperative research centers. The National Institutes of Health should receive more funding for basic biomedical research. Universities can strengthen the patent positions of its researchers to better compete. The U.S. government could stimulate private R&D by providing or guaranteeing low-interest loans for high risk R&D. It could also guarantee government purchase of certain products where R&D is stymied by market uncertainties. Finally, the Department of Commerce should expand its role of strategist for the nation's research-based businesses. There is nothing anti-democratic about having a targeted strategy for the nation's research-based industry. This does not imply collusion or violate free-market principles. The Department of Commerce is the one agency that can fill this role, which is merely an expansion of its current role of promoter of industry-wide RDLPs. The U.S. government can set targets and encourage industry along the dimensions of those targets. In a competitive international economy where the other contenders are all taking advantage of government planning and coordination, it is to the benefit of the United States to consider measures to take advantage of the efficiencies of government targeting.

11   Some Implications

The existence of entrepreneurial science in America today requires that industry make some major adjustments in the way it supports and commercializes research. One of the most important realizations is that the truly innovative research is not likely to come out of the mammoth laboratory buildings that some of the larger companies have built. The atmosphere of the large corporation, as discussed earlier in this book, is not conducive to attracting, supporting, and maintaining the best scientists. The leading researchers will continue to be found at the university and the small entrepreneurial company. They will remain at the university for the prestige and independence which that type of institution confers. They will be found at the entrepreneurial company because this type of institution fosters creative science with a high degree of independence and the promise of lucrative rewards. The large corporation should not focus on being entrepreneurial. Instead, it should focus on linking with the entrepreneurial scientists in universities and startup firms. Although a number of large companies have grown to realize this fact, many corporations continue to place their confidence in their own laboratories for breakthrough research. It is better to train management in methods of spotting and making agreements with universities and entrepreneurial firms.

Chief executives and financial officers of large industrial firms should pay renewed attention to the entrepreneurial company. In biotechnology the startup has attracted investment because it offers various windows on technology. It is a mistake to limit investments to this criterion. First of all, investments in startups will prove to be good business because the climate is good for those startups to flourish. Secondly, the entrepreneurial firm provides far more than windows on technology. It provides centers for technology development. Expect that as entrepreneurial firms grow they will extend their research from the laboratory to the small scale-up phase. This will allow the company to retain a greater amount of royalties and control over the process leading to manufacture of the final product. Large corporations should recognize this trend and support the companies that are capable of taking this extra step in technology development for them. Large corporations should also focus on becoming better negotiators for technology, purchasing as much technology as possible for each process. Chief executives of entrepreneurial companies should plan carefully how much technology they want to give away for the corporate dollar. Just as it is in the interest of the large corporation to take as much technology as it can get, it is in the interest of the entrepreneurial company to give away as little technology as possible.

Negotiators of the technology for both the large and entrepreneurial firms should be aware that agreements signed on a developing technology may not be sufficient to guarantee accomplishment of all works and granting of all rights because of unforseen changes in the technology. Problems are generated when the people who sign the original agreements leave for another company, only to be replaced by new managers who have different expectations for the developing technology. This is an area where some degree of corporate trust and goodwill has to be established.

Chief executives of entrepreneurial firms should decide early in the firm's development whether it should be a target for acquisition. The small company should be positioned either to be acquired, to become an intermediary company, or to become a fully integrated research and manufacturing company. In biotechnology many of the firms would like to become fully integrated companies, but the economics of manufacturing and product testing in many cases will preclude this. Small companies would be wise to position themselves to be purchased if they don't reach certain performance benchmarks.

Research universities should become more of a focus for industrial involvement as universities become more capable of generating good research and trained personnel for industry. Expect increased competition on campus for the privilege of supporting research or initiating university-industrial programs. Corporations should not limit themselves to contract research opportunities. As the value of good technical manpower increases, competition for these trained scientists will increase. Corporations should support research that will yield basic developments that may have no immediate product implications. This is a difficult investment to make because the results cannot be calculated on a spreadsheet. It is nevertheless worthwhile for future opportunities to commercialize research, form joint arrangements with university scientists, and recruit top scientists out of the university.

In an international economy the value to America of increasing its basic research base cannot be stressed too strongly. In addition to supporting research on campus with grants and exchanges, large research corporations should lobby in Washington to increase support for research universities through the National Institutes of Health, the National Science Foundation and other agencies charged with grant-giving to universities. It is also in the interest of the large corporation for Congress to pass legislation that will help foster development of the high-technology startups. These startups will provide the technological edge needed to compete with European and Japanese firms. Take advantage of the unique triumvirate of the large corporation-university-entrepreneurial firm and support any legislation that will strengthen the bonds.

Within the culture of the large corporation it is important to foster innovation. However, with the new recognition of the advantages of working with entrepreneurial firms, there is less of a need for so-called intrapreneurial programs. Let's face it: large corporations do many things well, but they don't act like small companies. If corporations persist in intrapreneuring, they should decentralize when possible, give as much autonomy to the divisions as possible, and provide generous equity rewards for achievement.

Several new implications follow for financial officers from the existence of entrepreneurial science. Since entrepreneurial science is fostered by the venture capital industry, it would be wise for financial executives to consider investments in venture capital funds. In addition to being sound investments, they contribute to the rate of innovation in this country. Financial officers and chief executives should also take a look at what limited partnership investments in cooperative research can do for the corporation. Limited partnerships greatly reduce the risk of research investment, don't reflect poorly on the company's balance sheet, and provide capital for research projects that might not otherwise be funded. They effectively stretch the research capacity of the corporation. It would be especially wise to examine the case histories of Becton Dickinson and Genentech in more detail to determine whether other companies qualify for the benefits of the limited partnership. Study the changes in the new tax law to determine how opportunities for research and development limited partnerships have changed. Look to Merrill Lynch and other financial giants for instruction on how blind pool limited partnerships can be of benefit to the corporation.

Chief executives from large, research-based companies should examine new and innovative ways to link up with both universities and entrepreneurial companies. Perhaps the Engenics model is worth examining in greater detail. In this model, arrangements were simultaneously made with a startup and two important research universities, enabling the founding companies to invest in both the basic and applied aspects of technology while linking the two aspects.

There are other ways to profit from investment in university research, such as endorsing regional technology development centers. Ground-floor investment or joint arrangements contribute to the local economy while providing new basic and applied research opportunities. In addition to contracts and product sales, these centers will provide valuable opportunities for personnel training and recruitment. Examine how states like Maryland and New Jersey offer opportunities for both entrepreneurial companies and established, research-based companies in the pharmaceutical, chemical, microelectronics, advanced ceramics and other industries.

University administrators have a lot to gain by paying attention to the growth of entrepreneurial science. They should be willing to gamble on starting up companies based upon university technology. Since most universities do not have experience in this area, it is wise to form good relationships with venture capital firms. Universities should consider the pros and cons of investing in their own ventures or in the venture capital funds that finance ventures arising from university research. Universities should also explore the option of inviting companies that invest in their research to invest in spin-off companies. University administrators should examine other ways to capitalize upon the trend of professors working in startups. Instead of fighting this trend, the university can profit if it encourages sensible interactions that don't interfere with the main job of the professor and his staff. Studying Yale's Science Park and the planning that went behind this project will help determine if this is the route that other universities should take.

Chief executives and corporate planners in research-based industries should take seriously the Japanese and European competition and work together with competitors to broaden the base in science and technology in this country. Look to the Department of Commerce for help in providing the models for such types of interaction and acting as mediators for competition. The Department of Commerce can also provide valuable information about the use of research and development limited partnerships to fund joint research activities. Industry should also carefully examine the trends in the microelectronics industry, where the competition from Japanese manufacturers has been taken into account.

Marketing executives should take notice of how entrepreneurial firms plan their new product development, taking their cue from the scientific work. There should be more marketing pull on the science. One way to accomplish this is to decentralize marketing in line with research, establishing marketing relationships that require new product innovation. This will combat the tendency for marketing executives to rely upon the proven products.

Research directors should examine whether it would be fruitful to make a large-scale arrangement with one or more universities to quickly boost the research capacities of the corporation. Careful study of the Monsanto-Washington University deal will help determine whether this is a proper direction for other companies. Research directors should also examine whether it would be desirable to carve up research laboratories into smaller units. By decentralizing research the research director may produce a more entrepreneurial climate for innovation. Research managers should also investigate government programs for cooperative research. Contacting the National Science Foundation will determine whether a program exists to serve a manager's needs. Many of these programs are structured to fund research that is too expensive for one company to fund.

Location of a company's research facilities is an important factor in technology transfer. As we stressed earlier in this book, technology is more likely to be transferred from the university to the corporation if the university scientist is physically close to the corporate scientist. It follows that the corporate scientist is less likely to visit university labs if his company is located far from the university. One solution is to move research laboratories to industrial parks located near campus. This relocation allows for a number of different types of technology transfer to take place. For example, the university scientist is close enough to monitor corporate projects. Arrangements can also be made where a number of corporate scientists can work in university laboratories without damaging their work in progress in the corporation. Research directors should also examine current models of personnel training by university researchers. Examine how Hoechst and DuPont enable their scientists to be trained by some of the world's finest university researchers.

In conclusion, it is to every party's benefit to recognize that the links between the university, the entrepreneurial company and the large corporation are growing stronger and that more opportunities will exist in the future for linking these institutions. We are witnessing a reorganization of the process of conducting and commercializing research. Companies that heed this trend are more likely to profit from it.

12   A View of the Future

The American economy is in a precarious position. The huge trade deficit, the government's failure to balance its own budget, and the loss of many of its traditional industries to foreign manufacturers point toward a troubled economy. One answer to these dilemmas is to innovate old industries, converting our old factories into robot- and computer-oriented factories of the future that can be capable of retooling and shifting assembly operations for new products as markets shift. The "intelligent factory" depends upon the abilities of high technologies to develop in this country. Products addressing new markets and replacing other products in established markets depend upon the ingenuity of entrepreneurial science, the ability to discover and transfer scientific and engineering results quickly and efficiently. Manufacturing methods for the intelligent factory rely upon entrepreneurial science for process development. Since we can no longer compete well in many traditional manufacturing systems because labor is cheaper in foreign countries, we must become increasingly more reliant upon creativity and innovation. We must take advantage of our world's leadership in science if we are to ensure a sound economy for future generations.

One method of helping entrepreneurial science benefit society is in the development of the small entrepreneurial firms such as those that we have investigated in biotechnology. These should be encouraged in other high-technology industries as well. Forming linkages between the university laboratory and the world of industrial production requires that financial rewards and investment money both be made available. The small company plays a crucial role in bridging the gap between the two cultures of the university and the large corporation. Large corporations recognize that the innovative talent is found in the small corporation and that the small corporation is much more receptive to a formal and commercial relationship than the university. In Centocor, Engenics, and BioTechnica International we have seen three methods of forming those linkages. It is especially important to note how the formation of satellite companies can occur when the biotech firm matures. These companies can offer new equity opportunities and excitement for researchers and businessmen. The limited partnership is another vehicle to stimulate innovation while helping to finance the growth of new companies. Both of these phenomena rely upon the availability of investment capital, which in turn points towards the tax structure in this country. Even though the new tax laws discourage private investors from investing in these enterprises, expect that there will be increasing amounts of institutional venture capital money available for high-technology startups. New technologies such as advanced robotics, artificial intelligence, and fiber optics should blossom, providing the materials for manufacturing innovation in some of our smokestack industries while creating entirely new industries. The U.S. government should alter its tax policies to ensure that venture capital money is available for this badly needed innovation.

These trends will lead to further commercialization of the university, which has suffered from decreased government funding of research. Commercialization will come primarily through deals completed by small companies with university researchers. Some of the funding burden for universities should and will be borne by state governments, which now see high technology as crucial for their local economic development programs. There is little doubt that research contracts by large corporations and entrepreneurial firms to universities will shape university research, just as the government grant-giving system shapes research. It will not cut down on basic research for the sake of applied research, but it will add a sharper focus to basic research; implications for applied research will be considered in these programs, so the research will not be done simply for the advancement of knowledge.

Expect to see more linkages between the university, the small company, and the large corporation, with the small corporation acting as a kind of technology middleman. The university will be increasingly receptive to these links with the corporate world, especially as basic research funding by the government is cut. Small companies will become even more adept at contacting and contracting with universities. These companies should continue, in turn, to be rewarded in the public markets, which have already poured large amounts of money into these firms.

In light of the crisis in government funding, universities must become increasingly aware of commercial opportunities for spin-off companies and technology licensing. The very best research universities with a theoretical approach to their science may not seek equity from spin-offs in the near future, but expect that the universities that seek application of research will insist upon some play in the entrepreneurial spin-off from university research. Every major research university will have to contend with the tendency for the researcher to be lured away from his lab into the corporation. Yale is a forerunner for other top universities that will have to provide incubator facilities near campus and work out arrangements for faculty members to continue their university duties while being involved in entrepreneurial companies.

If assessments by the Department of Commerce are correct, expect increasing interest by industries in doing pro-competitive research. This trend should continue to be encouraged by the department. The trend may or may not compete with the university as a research channel, depending upon how it is managed. Some pro-competitive agreements may involve contract research with universities on the scale of the Semiconductor Research Corporation, boosting the number of linkages between the university and industry. As the competitive effects of Japanese and European high technology planning become apparent, American corporate leaders should rush to raise the level of technology in this country through consortia in the way that the microelectronics industry has responded to its crisis. Perhaps some industrial leaders will have the foresight to plan consortia before they're faced with stifling competition from abroad.

Government planning by Japan, West Germany, and the United Kingdom will continue in high technology as will broad-based coordination between members of the European Economic Community. Planning and coordination have been particularly successful in Japan, where the country has made impressive progress in microelectronics and computer-oriented industries. There are no plans in the Reagan administration for the government to plan industrial production, although the Department of Commerce is making some progress in encouraging research cooperatives for pro-competitive research. Lack of planning is a serious gap in our free enterprise system. The Department of Commerce should be allowed to help shape an industrial policy without telling individual companies what they can or can't do. This shaping would take the form of voluntary, industry-wide guidelines, goals for the manufacture of certain products, and corresponding basic research goals.

The federal government must supply badly needed research money to fund the basic research at universities, primarily through the National Institutes of Health and the National Science Foundation. Transferring technology from the university to the corporation is one thing that America does best. We have built our lead in biotechnology, for example, based upon the university research on basic mechanisms. This support must increase if we are to maintain our lead in the face of government-planned efforts in Japan and other countries. The government could also offer greater stimulus for entrepreneurial science by structuring tax laws to encourage risky investment in small firms. With the 1986 tax law it now seems that the government is headed in the wrong direction regarding these policies.

The federal government must make increasing efforts to interest students in science and engineering, providing the human resources for entrepreneurial science. The NSF's engineering research centers should play a valuable role here. The state governments ought to take more responsibility for training students at state universities and providing opportunities for students to get a taste of industry through summer work programs and internships with corporations. Consistent with the decentralization of government which was one of Reagan's mandates during his election, the state government should take increasing responsibility for regional development by creating new bridges between industry, academia, and state government. State governments are assuming that luring high technology into their regions will do more than create new jobs in those industries; it will boost the feeder industries, leading to more employment and greater revenues. One criticism of state government programs is that they don't tend to be market-oriented. States must know specifically why they should attract what types of industry, fitting the new industry to the other industrial needs and strengths in the region. For example, if New York State were to benefit most from biotechnology's application to agriculture, it should give this priority over biopharmaceutical companies. As it stands, state governments tend to be fairly general about the types of industries they want to attract. They must learn to target their industries.

As the university becomes more sophisticated about assessing and promoting its own spin-off technology, expect that the role of the technology transfer company such as Research Corporation will change. Universities are finding that they are capable of handling the patenting and licensing procedures. As the revenues become more attractive, the universities will build their technology tranfer capabilities and offer the convenience of an on-campus location for the university scientist. Research Corporation must continue to respond to this trend, cooperating more actively and closely with university patent administrators in handling the disclosures that patent administrators want to give over to the firm. Administrators will use Research Corporation to boost their marketing power rather than using it as a substitute for in-house work.

The commercialization of the university will make it more reliant upon the goodwill of large corporations who donate equipment and supplies to the university. The university will be more eager to be the recipient of the research grant given in exchange for patent licensing rights and other benefits. The commercialization of the university and the increased knowledge that industries have about the capabilities and location of scientists will yield increased contract research and other types of interactions. Expect that as a result of this commercialization, there will be a greater flow of personnel from the university into the corporation and vice versa. The commercialization of the university through contact with industry should be encouraged by both parties. Our higher educational system, the spring from which industry draws, needs money and equipment at a time of government austerity.

In the area of finance, the limited partnership blind pools will exert an effect upon entrepreneurial science, providing needed money and money management to high-technology firms. As the general partner, the financial corporation will be in a role where it can influence the direction of research and development. If it continues, for financial reasons, to insist upon product development within a two- to three-year time frame, this will affect the types of products coming out of entrepreneurial companies. These firms will be able to use some of the revenues from the limited partnership to fund longer-term research. Expect that the tax reform will make it more difficult for high-tech companies to find investors for their own limited partnerships. The limited partnership should be saved; it's a valuable instrument for entrepreneurial science.

Entrepreneurial science should be encouraged at all levels of government and industry because it is the key to product innovation, the most dynamic aspect of the economy. The experimentation of the 1980's in new linkages between universities, government, and industry should prove to be fruitful to the way business is conducted in the United States. A new industrial revolution has begun, a research revolution that the United States cannot afford to ignore. Our capacity to compete in the new international economy and our ability to innovate products and manufacturing processes depends upon the efficient transfer of entrepreneurial science.

Notes

3. Large Companies Look to the University

1. Lois S. Peters, and Herbert Fusfeld, *Current U.S. University Industry Research Connections*, National Science Foundation Report NSB 82-2, 1982, 52.

4. The Universities: Allies with Industry

1. Ibid., 83.

5. Federal and State Assistance for High Technology

1. U.S. Congressional Office of Technology Assessment, *Technology, Innovation and Regional Economic Development* (Washington, D.C.: U.S. Congressional Office of Technology Assessment, July 1984), 116.
2. Ibid., 141.

9. The Research and Development Limited Partnership: Potentials and Problems

1. Lois S. Peters, and Herbert Fusfeld, *Research and Development Limited Partnerships (RDLPs) and Their Significance for Innovation* (New York: New York University), 53.

10. Government Strategies in R&D: A Comparison

1. National Science Foundation *International Science and Technology Update* (Washington, D.C.: National Science Foundation, January, 1985), 212.

2. U.S. General Accounting Office, *Support for Development of Electronics and Materials Technologies by the Governments of the United States, Japan, West Germany, France and the United Kingdom* (Washington, D.C.: U.S. General Accounting Office), 5.

3. National Science Foundation, 35.

4. Ibid., 46.

5. Eric Bloch, "Basic Research and Economic Health: The Coming Challenge," *Science*, May 2, 1986, 597.

6. Mark D. Dibner, "Biotechnology in Europe," *Science*, June 13, 1986, 1367.

7. Japan Economic Institute, *JEI Report* (Washington, D.C.: Japan Economic Institute), February 7, 1986, 18.

8. U.S. Congressional Office of Technology Assessment, *Commercial Biotechnology: An International Analysis* Washington, D.C., January 1984, 514.

9. Ibid., 307.

Bibliography

Abelson, Philip H. "Evolving State-University-Industry Relations." *Science*, January 24, 1986, 317.

American Glass Review. "Competition in the search for a new glass container." April 1985, 7–18.

Anderson, Laurie. "High Tech Park Takes Off." *Knickerbocker News*, March 25, 1985, 1.

Aronson, James M., and Alimansky, Burt. "Funding new technologies with research and development limited partnerships." *American Society of Mechanical Engineers*, February 17, 1985.

Association of American Universities. *University Policies on Conflict of Interest and Delay of Publication.* Washington, D.C.: Association of American Universities, February 1985.

Atchison, Sandra. "Meet the Campus Capitalists of Bionic Valley." *Business Week*, May 5, 1986, 114–115.

Bartlett, Joseph W., and Siera, James V. "Research and Development Limited Partnerships as a Device to Exploit University Owned Technology." *Journal of College and University Law*, vol. 10, no. 4, Spring 1983–1984.

Battelle Columbus Laboratories. *Development of High Technology Industries in New York State.* Columbus, Ohio: Battelle Columbus Laboratories, 1982.

———. *Guided Wave Optoelectronics Manufacturing Technology Development Program.* Columbus: Battelle Columbus Laboratories, April 1984.

Bell Communications Research. *1984 Annual Review.* Bell Communications Research, 1985.

Ben Franklin Partnership Fund Board. *Ben Franklin Advanced Technology*

Center: Annual Report, 1983–1984. Ben Franklin Partnership Fund Board, 1985.

———. *Ben Franklin Partnership Challenge Grant Programs for Technological Innovation.* Ben Franklin Partnership Board, February 1985.

Berg, Eric. "New Phone Research Giant." *New York Times*, July 15, 1985, D1.

Bloch, Eric. "Basic Research and Economic Health: The Coming Challenge." *Science*, May 2, 1986, 595–599.

Blumenthal, David, Gluck, Michael, et. al. "University-Industry Research Relationships in Biotechnology: Implications for the University." *Science*, June 13, 1986.

Business Week, "An Idea That's Working: Federal Funds for High Tech Start-ups." October 22, 1984, 146A–146D.

Cape, Ronald. "On Deserving Awe and Envy." *Bio/Technology*, October 1984.

———. "Who Will You Blame When the Other Guy Wins." *Bio/Technology*, April 1986, 368.

Centocor, Inc. *Annual Report 1985.* Malvern, Pa.: Centocor, Inc., 1986.

Ceramic Industry. "Industry Invests $5 Million for Stronger, Lighter Glass." July 1985, 34–36.

Chemical Week, "New Ways to get Industry to Academe." July 4, 1984.

———. "Scientist Superstar in a New Role." December 12, 1984.

Clark, Evert. "Passing the Buck in R&D Financing." *Business Week*: December 2, 1985, 34.

Commission of the European Communities. "Towards a European Technology Community." Brussels: Commission of the European Communities, June 25, 1985.

Commonwealth of Massachusetts. *Massachusetts Technology Development Corporation Annual Report 1984.* Commonwealth of Massachusetts, 1985.

Crawford, Mark. "Biotech Market Changing Rapidly." *Science*, January 3, 1986, 12–14.

———. "Industry Wary of Tech Transfer Bills." *Science*, June 7, 1985, 1182.

Culliton, Barbara J. "Monsanto Gives Washington U. $23.5 Million." *Science*, June 18, 1982, 1295–1296.

Cutter, Leslie S. "The University of Connecticut Health Center Research and Development Corporation." Master's Thesis, Hartford Graduate Center.

Dibner, Mark D. "Biotechnology in Europe." *Science*, June 13, 1986, 1367–1372.

Donaldson, Lufkin & Jenrette. *Cytogen.* New York: Donaldson, Lufkin & Jenrette, June 1986.

Esch, Mary. "RPI Aids Young Companies in its 3-Part Drive for High Tech Environment." *Schenectady Gazette*, July 28, 1983.

Fischer, Donald. "Venturing Capital." *Financial Planning*, March 1985, 130–135.

Gas Research Institute. *1986–1990 Research and Development Plan: Executive Summary.* Gas Research Institute, June 1985.

———. *Annual Report 1984.* Gas Research Institute, 1985.

Gibson, G. Thomas. "How R&D Pools Fund Add-On Businesses." *Venture*, March 1984, 17.

Grounds, Preston W. *University-Industry Interaction Guide to Developing Fundamental Research Contracts.* Allentown, Pa.: Council for Chemical Research, 1985.

Hamilton, Joan. "Biotech's First Superstar." *Business Week*, April 14, 1986, 68–72.

Hancock, Elise. "Academe Meets Industry: Charting the Bottom Line." *Johns Hopkins Magazine*, August 1983, 1–9.

Kezerian, Steve. "Cooperative Research: The Link to Industry." *Yale Magazine*, December 1985, 16–22.

Langfitt, Thomas W., Hackney, Sheldon, et al. *Partners in the Research Enterprise.* Philadelphia: University of Pennsylvania Press, 1982.

Lederman, Leon M. "The Value of Fundamental Science." *Scientific American*, November 1984, 40–47.

Martin, John and Kensinger, John. "An Economic Analysis of R&D Limited Partnerships." *Midland Corporate Finance Journal*, vol. 3, No. 4, Winter 1986.

McCurdy, Patrick. "CCR Does Something About the Weather." *Chemical Week*, July 4, 1984.

Mensch, Gerhard O. *Stalemate in Technology.* Cambridge, Mass.: Ballinger Publishing Co., 1984.

Merrifield, D. Bruce. "Forces of Change Affecting High Technology Industries." *National Journal*, January 29, 1983.

Moss, Thomas H. "Industry-University Research Partnerships: Resolution of Conflicts." San Francisco: American Physical Society Symposium on University/Industry Partnerships, November 21, 1983.

National Governors' Association. *Technology and Growth: State Initiatives in Technological Innovation.* Washington, D.C.: National Governors' Association, October 1983.

National Science Foundation. *Cooperative Science: A National Study of University and Industry Researchers.* Washington, D.C.: National Science Foundation, November 1984.

———. *Corporate Science: A National Study of University and Industry Researchers.* Washington, D.C.: National Science Foundation, 1984.

———. *Development of University-Industry Cooperative Research Centers.* Washington, D.C.: National Science Foundation, 1984.

———. *Directorate for Engineering Program Descriptions.* Washington, D.C.: National Science Foundation, April 2, 1985.

———. *NSF Program Solicitation—Small Business Innovation Research.* Washington, D.C.: National Science Foundation, 1985, 1–39.

———. *University-Industry Research Relationships.* Washington, D.C.: National Science Foundation, 1982.

National Science Foundation News. "102 Firms Receive NSF Awards for Small Business Innovation Research." 1–11.

New York State Science and Technology Foundation. *New York State Centers for Advanced Technology.* Albany: New York State Science and Technology Foundation.

North Carolina Biotechnology Center. *Developing the Biotechnology Component of Engineering: Needs and Opportunities.* Research Triangle Park: North Carolina Biotechnology Center, September 1983.

———. *Triangle Universities Consortium for Research and Education in Plant Molecular Biology: Description of the Fellowship Program.* Research Triangle Park: North Carolina Biotechnology Center, August 1984.

Personal Investor. "Brave New Deals." November 1985, 22–30.

Petillon, Lee R., and Hall, Robert Joe. *R&D Partnerships: Structuring the Transaction.* Clark Boardman Company, Ltd., 1985.

Petkevich, J. Misha, and MacCallum, David H. *Centocor.* Hambrecht and Quist, May 6, 1986, 1–16.

Phalon, Richard. "University as Venture Capitalist." *Forbes,* December 19, 1983, 82–93.

Posner, Bruce G. "Strategic Alliances." *Inc.,* June 1985, 74–80.

Prudential Bache Securities. *Prutech II Research and Development Partnership.* Prudential Bache Securities.

Rensselaer Polytechnic Institute. *Research at Rensselaer.* Troy, N.Y.: Rensselaer Polytechnic Institute.

Research Corporation. *Research Corporation Report, 1984* Tucson, Ariz.: Research Corporation, 1985.

Sanger, David E. "U.S. and Companies Set Campus Centers for Supercomputers." *The New York Times,* February 26, 1985, 1.

Schmitt, Rolannd. "Successful Corporate R&D." *Harvard Business Review,* May–June 1985, 124–128.

Schulman, Roger. "Reagan and Foreign Rivalry Light a Fire Under Spending." *Business Week,* July 8, 1985, 86–104.

Singer, Dale. "Monsanto, Washington U. Pleased by Success of Venture." *St. Louis Post-Dispatch,* February 4, 1985.

Smith, Emily T., "Monsanto's College Alliance is Getting High Marks." *Business Week*, May 12, 1986, 33–34.

Spalding, R. J. "Why the Industry is Slow to Enter Joint Research." *Chemical Week*, May 15, 1985, 62–66.

State of New Jersey. *Report of the Governor's Commission on Science and Technology*. State of New Jersey, 1984.

Stombler, Milton P. *Guide to University-Industry Research Agreements*. Santa Monica: Society of Research Administrators, January 1984.

Sun, Marjorie. "The Japan Challenge in Biotechnology." *Science*, November 15, 1985, 789–792.

Teitelman, Robert. "Searching for Serendipity." *Forbes*, May 6, 1985, 80–81.

Tifft, Sara, "R&D Goes to College." *In Vivo*, 1985, 20–24.

University of California. *The Microelectronics Innovation and Computer Research (MICRO) Program*. Berkeley: University of California, January 31, 1984.

University Patents, Inc. *1985 Annual Report*. Westport, Conn.: University Patents, 1986.

U.S. Congressional Office of Technology Assessment. *Commercial Biotechnology: An International Analysis*. Washington, D.C.: U.S. Congressional Office of Technology Assessment, January 1984.

U.S. Congressional Office of Technology Assessment. *Technology, Innovation, and Regional Economic Development*. Washington, D.C.: U.S. Congressional Office of Technology Assessment, 1984.

U.S. Department of Commerce. *Examples Representative of FY 1985 Services, Products and Assistance to Small Business*. U.S. Department of Commerce, February 24, 1985.

———. *High Technology Industries: Profiles and Outlooks—Biotechnology*. Washington, D.C.: U.S. Deparment of Commerce, July 1984.

———. *Information and Steps Necessary to Form Research and Development Limited Partnerships*. Washington, D.C.: U.S. Department of Commerce, December 1983.

———. *The New Climate for Joint Research*. Washington, D.C.: U.S. Department of Commerce, May 1983.

———. *Research and Development Limited Partnerships: List of Specialists in RDLP's*. Washington, D.C.: U.S. Department of Commerce, October 1984.

———. *Research and Development Limited Partnerships: OPTI Collection of Institutional Sources*. Washington, D.C.: U.S. Department of Commerce, August 1984.

U.S. General Accounting Office. *Support for Development of Electronics and*

Materials Technologies by the Governments of the United States, Japan, West Germany, France, and the United Kingdom. Washington, D.C.: U.S. General Accounting Office, September 9, 1985.

U.S. Small Business Administration. *State Activities in Venture Capital, Early-Stage Financing, and Secondary Markets.* Washington, D.C.: U.S. Small Business Administration, May 1984.

Varrin, Robert D., and Kirkich, Diane S. "Guidelines for Industry-Sponsored Research at Universities." *Science*, January 25, 1985, 385–388.

Webber, David. "Chief Scientist Schneiderman: Monsanto's Love Affair with R&D." *Chemical and Engineering News*, December 24, 1984, 6–13.

Webra, Philip. "Federal Financial Support for High Technology Industries." Washington, D.C.: *Congressional Budget Office*, June, 1985.

Weiss, Gary. "Selling Science." *Barron's.* July, 22, 1985, 20–24.

White, Lawrence J. "Clearing the Legal Path to Cooperative Research." *Technology Review*, July 1985.

Wilson, James E. "Rewarding Investors." *Venture*, October 1985, 37–38.

Index

ABC (American Broadcasting Corporation), 76-77
Academic freedom, 25, 28, 31, 42, 87
Advanced Technology Center of Southeastern Pennsylvania (University City Science Center), 62
Advanced Television Research Program (MIT), 76
Affiliates/subsidiaries, 9-10, 14-15. *See also* name of specific affiliate or subsidiary
Agricultural Genetics Co. (United Kingdom), 122
Agriculture, U.S. Department of, 60-61
Agrigenetics Research Associates Limited, 18, 112
Airco Industrial Gases, 64
Alafi-Washington Company (Alafi Capital and Washington University), 90
Alcoa, 37
Allied Corporation, 26-27
Alpert, A. Sidney, 82
American Cyanamid Company, 98
American Telephone & Telegraph, 51, 77

Ampex, 76-77
Analytical Biosystems Inc. (Brown University), 91-92
Antitrust issues, 72-73
Applied Biosystems, 82
Applied Molecular Genetics, 53
Applied research, 32, 46, 119, 121, 122, 124, 125
Arizona, University of, 81
Arizona State University, 26
AT&T (American Telephone & Telegraph), 51, 77
Australia, 76

Bacon, Stevenson, 83-84
Basic research, 25-26, 28, 31, 46, 83-85, 88, 118, 120-21, 129, 134-36. *See also* Pro-competitive research
Battelle Memorial Laboratories, 76
Baylor College of Medicine, 86-87
BBL Microbiology Systems, 98
BCM Technologies, 86-87
Becton, Dickinson and Company, ˙64, 105-6, 130
Bellcore, 77
Bell Laboratories, 77
Bendix Corporation, 16

Ben Franklin Partnership Program
(Pennsylvania), 61-63
Berkeley, University of California
at, 26
Biogen, 24
Biomedical Research Park (Chicago), 53
Bio Polymers Inc. (University of
Connecticut), 89
Biotech, Inc., 8
BioTechnica, 9-12, 134
Biotechnology industry: advantages
of, 7-8; and affiliates/subsidiaries,
9-10; and corporate-university
partnerships, 7, 8-9, 12, 14-16,
16-17, 19; and corporations, 12,
13, 17-18, 128; creation of, 8-9;
financing of, 13, 14-15, 18, 95,
96-99, 101-2; future of, 11, 13,
18-19; international competition
in, 117-21, 122-23, 124-25; and
managerial talent, 9-12; as a
model for high technology business, 7-19; and new ventures, 95,
96-99, 101-2; problems of, 13;
and product development, 8, 12,
13, 14, 16; and risk taking, 17,
19; and scientific talent, 7, 8-9,
11, 13-14, 19; state support of,
54; and the stockmarket, 99; and
universities, 7, 8-9, 12, 14-17,
19, 23-26, 29, 30, 32; and venture capital, 7, 8-9. See also name
of specific organization, program,
and state
Biotechnology Investments Limited
(BIL), 95-96
Bio-technology Research Park
(Worcester, Massachusetts), 68-69
Blair, James, 95-96, 99, 101
Blind pool partnership, 99-100, 130,
137

Bloch, Eric, 50, 116-17
Boeing Corporation, 37
Bok, Derek, 46
Borrus, Michael, 73
Bristol-Myers, 42, 97
Brown University, 91-92
Buffalo, State University of New
York at, 66-67

California, University of, 16-17, 26,
50, 51, 106
California Institute of Technology,
27
California (state), 54, 67-68
Canada, 76
Cape, Ronald, 120-21
Carey, Hugh, 38
Carnegie-Mellon University, 62
Caruthers, Marvin, 82
Case Western Reserve University,
87-89
Celanese Corporation, 41-42
Celltech (United Kingdom),
122
Center for Advanced Research in
Biotechnology (University of
Maryland), 59-60
Center for Advanced Technology
(CAT-New York State), 34, 66-67
Center for Advanced Television
Studies (CATS), 76-77
Center for Agricultural Biotechnol-
ogy (University of Maryland), 60-
61
Center for Biotechnology in Agricul-
ture (Cornell University), 67
Center for Biotechnology Research
(CBR-Engenics), 16
Center for Ceramics Research (Rut-
gers University), 57
Center for Food Technology (Rut-
gers University), 57

Center for Industrial Innovation
  (RPI), 37
Center for Integrated Electronics
  (RPI), 38
Center for Integrated Systems (Stan-
  ford), 44-45
Center for Interactive Computer
  Graphics (RPI), 37, 38
Center for Manufacturing Productiv-
  ity and Technology Transfer
  (RPI), 37-38
Center for Marine Biotechnology
  (University of Maryland), 60
Center for Medical Biotechnology
  (University of Maryland), 61
Centers for Excellence (Massachu-
  setts), 68-69
Centocor, 14-16, 19, 99, 108-9, 134
Chapel Hill, University of North
  Carolina at, 63-64, 79. See also
  Research Triangle Park (Durham,
  North Carolina)
Charlotte, University of North Caro-
  lina at, 64
Chauncey, Henry, 43-44
Chemical industry, 26-27, 31, 78-
  79. See also specific company
Chicago Circle, University of Illinois
  at, 26
Ciba-Geigy, 65
Cleveland Advanced Manufacturing
  Program (Case Western Reserve),
  88
COBE Laboratories, 98
Cohen, Edward, 58
Colorado, University of, 60, 81
Colwell, Rita, 59
Columbia University, 27, 50, 66-67
Commerce, U.S. Department of, 52,
  75-76, 125, 131, 135-36
Community Development block
  grants (HUD), 53

Competition: biotechnology industry,
  117-21, 122-23, 124-25; interna-
  tional, 115-25, 129, 135-36, 138;
  microelectronics, 115-16, 117-18,
  120, 121, 122, 123, 124-25; for
  scientific talent, 128-29; for state
  support, 54-55. See also Europe;
  Germany, Federal Republic of;
  Japan; Pro-competitive research;
  United Kingdom; West Germany
Computer equipment. See Semicon-
  ductor industry
Computervision Corporation, 38
Conflict of interest, 85, 90-92, 93
Connecticut, University of, 89-90
Connecticut Product Development
  Corporation, 53-54
Consulting, 22
Contract research, 17-18, 27, 30,
  40-42, 97, 128, 135. See also
  Pro-competitive research
Cornell University, 23, 27, 32, 33-
  37, 51, 66-67
Corporate-university partnerships:
  advantages of, 2-3, 21-23, 47,
  133-34; and consulting, 22; and
  the federal government, 50-52; future of, 133-38; problems with,
  46-47; and pro-competitive research, 73; and scientific talent,
  21-22, 127, 131-32; as a source of
  university funding, 21-22, 28, 30-
  31; universities as initiators of,
  30. See also Biotechnology industry; R&D limited partnership;
  Venture capital
Corporation for Innovation Development Program (New York State),
  66
Corporations: and biotechnology industry, 12, 13, 17-18, 128; expenditures for R&D by, 2; influ-

Corporations (*Continued*)
  ence on U.S. economy of, 1-2;
  and innovation, 127, 129; international aspects of, 15; and marketing, 12, 15; and new ventures,
  95, 96, 97-99, 102, 127-28; and
  product development, 8, 12; and
  research parks, 27-28; response to
  growth of high tech business of,
  3, 4-5, 129; and risk taking, 8,
  12, 79; and subsidiaries, 14-15.
  See also Corporate-university partnerships; name of specific industry
  or company
Cottrell, Frederick Gardner, 83
Cottrell College Science Grants, 83
Cottrell Research Grants Program,
  83
Council for Chemical Research, 27,
  31, 78
Cray Corporation, 51
Creative Biomolecules, 18
Cyanamid, 27
Cytogen, 97, 98-99

Dana Farber Cancer Institute, 108
Data General, 37, 64
Defense, U.S. Department of, 75,
  123
DeFfigos, John, 67
Delaware, University of, 27, 50
Dianon, Inc., 15
Dibner, Mark, 119
Digital Equipment Corporation, 37,
  38, 45, 58
Drexel University, 62
Duke University, 63-64, 79, 108.
  See also Research Triangle Park
  (Durham, North Carolina)
DuPont, 46, 60-61, 65-66, 132
Dura, Michael, 108

Eastman Kodak, 27, 33-34, 37, 97,
  98

Economic Development Administra-
  tion, U.S., 53-54
Economic development bonds, 50,
  53
Economic Recovery Tax Act (1981),
  53
Edelman, Lawrence, 56-57
Edison Animal Biotechnology Center
  (Case Western Reserve), 88
Edison Polymer Innovation Corpora-
  tion (Case Western Reserve), 88
E. F. Hutton, 110
Electronics Development Center
  (DuPont), 65-66
Electric power industry, 77-78, 80
Elf Aquitaine, 16
Eli Lilly, 86-87, 97, 101
Engenics, 16-17, 130, 134
Engineering Research Centers
  (NSF), 50, 124, 136
England. *See* United Kingdom
Europe, 5, 40, 71, 78, 123, 131.
  See also name of specific country
European Strategic Program of Re-
  search and Development in Infor-
  mation Technology (ESPRIT),
  123
Evaluation of technology, 82-83, 84
Evans and Sutherland Corporation,
  86
Exxon Corporation, 21, 40, 51

Fairchild Semiconductor, 38, 45
Farmitalia Carlo Erba SpA, 98
Federal government: and biotechnology industry, 12; and corporate-
  university partnerships, 50-52; en-
  couragement of technology transfer by, 5, 50, 53, 88, 125, 131,
  135-36; loans and grants programs
  of, 50, 53-54; R&D role of, 115-
  25; risk-taking involvement of,
  125; and scientific talent, 50, 136;

and state support, 55. *See also* name of specific agency, department, or program
FMC Corporation, 14, 15
Food and Drug Administration, U.S., 13
Foreign competition. *See* Competition: international; name of specific country
Foreign corporations/money: investment of, 4, 25. *See also* name of specific country
For-profit venture companies, 88-89, 91
Forrestal Center (Princeton), 27
Forsyth Dental Center, 9, 10
France, 115, 123, 124
Fusfeld, Herbert, study by, 21, 30-31, 33, 103-4, 105-6, 110, 112

Gas Research Institute, 78
GCE/IC Systems, 64
Genentech, 18, 24, 106-8, 130
General Electric Company, 37, 38, 45, 64, 69
General Foods, 16, 33-34
General Motors, 37
Genetic Systems, 97
Genex Corporation, 14, 17, 24
Germany, Federal Republic of, 122
Glick, J. Leslie, 14
Good Year Research, 26
Gould/AMI, 45
Governor's Commission on Science and Technology (New Jersey), 56, 57, 58
Grace, W.R., 40-41
Gregory, Gene, 120
GTE, 45

Hambrecht & Quist, 15, 107, 110
Hardy, Ralph, 9, 11-12
Harris Semiconductor, 38

Harvard University, 24, 46, 50, 90
Hewlett Packard, 45
High-technology business: advantages of, 3, 4; biotechnology industry as a model for, 7-19; and explosion of scientific knowledge, 2-3; as a panacea for U.S. economy, 2, 4, 5. *See also* Biotechnology industry; Microelectronics industry; New ventures; Pro-competitive research; name of specific industry, organization, or program
Hodges, Luther, 63
Hoechst AG, 25, 27, 132
Hoffman-La Roche, 14
Hohnke, Lyle, 89-90
Holman, Robert, 76
Honeywell, 26, 45
Howard, William, 26, 74
Hybritech, 97, 101

IBM (International Business Machines), 37, 38, 43, 45, 51, 63-64
Illinois, University of, 26, 51, 81
Illinois Institute of Technology, 26
Immunorex Associates, 15
Incubator concept, 34-35, 39, 43-44, 53, 57-58, 62, 135
Industrial collegia, 40
Industrial Liaison Program (MIT), 39-40
Industrial Revenue Bonds, 53
Industrial Technology Institute (Michigan), 69-70
Industrial Technology Partnership program (U.S. Department of Commerce), 52
Industry/University Cooperative Research Centers Program [NSF], 51
Industry/University Cooperative Research Projects Program (NSF), 50

Information sharing. *See* Pro-com-
petitive research
Inman, Bobby, 71-73, 74
Innovation partnerships. *See* Corpo-
rate-university partnerships; R&D
limited partnership
Intel, 45
International competition. *See* Com-
petition: international; name of
specific country
International Partners in Glass Re-
search, 76
Intrapreneuring, 3, 129
Investment banking industry, 3-4.
See also Stockmarket and new
ventures; Venture capital
Invitron, 24
ITT (International Telephone &
Telegraph), 45

Jackson, William M., 91-92
Japan: and biotechnology industry,
117-20, 125; compared to U.S.,
115-16, 119-21; competition from,
2, 5, 23, 113, 115, 123, 124,
125, 131; expenditures for R&D
by, 115, 116, 117-20; and joint
venture in glass research, 76; MIT
educational programs in, 40; overview of, 117-21; and pro-competitive research, 71, 73, 74, 76-77,
78, 79; and semiconductor industry, 23, 72, 117-18, 120; universities in, 75, 121
Johns Hopkins University, 60
Johnson & Johnson, 8, 25-26, 27,
98
Johnston Associates, 8, 98
John von Neumann Center (near
Princeton), 51, 58
Joint Institute for Laboratory Astro-
physics (University of Colorado
and University of Maryland), 60

Kiley, Thomas, 107, 108
Kleiner Perkins Caufield, 101
Klotz, Lynn, 9, 10-11
Koppers, 16
Ku, Kathy, 90

Laidlow Technology Venture Part-
ners, 110
Leahey, Duke, 90
Leder, Philip, 46
LeMaistre, Chris, 37
Linville, John, 45
Lockheed Corporation, 51
Low, George, 38
Lowell, University of, 69
Lubrizol, 18

MacCordy, Edward, 23-24
MacDonald, Nowell, 35-36, 74
McGrath, Paul J., 73
McKearn, Thomas, 98
Mahoney, Jerry, 39
Mailey, Tom, 34-35
Management: in biotechnology in-
dustry, 9-12; of new ventures, 96;
of patents, 81-85
Maryland, University of, 50, 58-61
Maryland Biotechnology Institute
(University of Maryland), 58-59
Maryland (state), 58-61, 130
Massachusetts, University of, 27,
68-69
Massachusetts Center of Excellence
Corporation, 69
Massachusetts General Hospital, 14,
25, 108
Massachusetts Institute of Technol-
ogy, 23, 27, 39-41, 50, 76
Massachusetts (state), 54, 68-69
Massachusetts Technology Develop-
ment Corporation, 53-54
Massachusetts Technology Park Cor-
poration, 69

Max-Planck-Institut fur Molekulare Genetik (Germany), 14, 108

MCNC. *See* Microelectronics Center of North Carolina

Mead, 16

Medical College of Pennsylvania, 81

Medicine and Dentistry of New Jersey, University of (UMDNJ), 56

Merrifield, D. Bruce, 52, 75, 106

Merrill Lynch, 100, 110, 130

Metropolitan Center for High Technology (Michigan), 70

Metz, E. David, 21, 22, 29, 75

Michigan Biotechnology Institute, 70

Michigan (state), 69-70

Microelectronics and Computer Technology Corporation (MCC), 27, 71-73, 77, 79, 80, 117

Microelectronics Center of North Carolina (MCNC), 64-65, 66

Microelectronics industry, 27, 115-18, 120, 121, 122, 123, 124-25. *See also* name of specific company

Microelectronics Innovation and Computer Research Opportunities Program (MICRO-California), 68

Microelectronics Research Program (West Germany), 122

Middlesex General-University Hospital (New Brunswick, New Jersey), 56

Monsanto Corporation, 23-25, 27, 45, 46, 60-61, 63, 69, 131

Morgan Stanley Ventures, 110

Moss, Thomas H., 87, 88

Motorola, 21, 22, 26, 45

Mullaney, William T., 86

Mycogen, 18

National Advanced Scientific Computing Centers (NSF), 51

National Aeronautics and Space Administration, 124

National Aquarium, 60

National Biotechnology Agency (Cape proposal), 121

National Bureau of Standards, 59-60, 124

National Cooperative Research Act (NCRA-1984), 52-53, 72-73, 75-76

National Governor's Association, 54-55

National Institutes of Health, 125, 129, 136

National Science Foundation: function of, 125; as information clearinghouse, 131; and pro-competitive research, 80; report by, 115-16; as a source of funding, 136

National Science Foundation support: for electronics research, 123-24; for Engineering Research Centers, 50, 124, 136; for Industry University Cooperative Research Centers Program, 51; for Industry/University Cooperative Research Projects Program, 50; for National Advanced Scientific Computing Centers, 51; for Small Business Innovation Research program, 52, 84-85, 124. *See also* name of specific center or university

National Semiconductor, 39

NEC Corporation, 119

Needleman, Philip, 24

New Enterprise Center (New Haven Science Park), 43

New Haven Science Park, 43-44, 53, 130-31

New Jersey Commission on Science and Technology, 57-58

New Jersey Institute of Technology, 57

New Jersey (state), 56-58, 130

New Jersey Venture Capital Partnership, 58

Newman, Joshua, 67-68

New ventures: and biotechnology industry, 95, 96-99, 101-2; and conflict of interest, 85, 90-92, 93; financing of, 95-102, 127-28; management of, 96; and patents, 88, 90, 100; and R&D limited partnerships, 95, 99-100, 102; and risk taking, 89, 98, 99, 101; and royalties, 83, 87, 89, 90, 93, 98, 99, 100; and scientific talent, 85-86, 96, 100; social effects of, 100-101; and the stockmarket, 95, 97, 99, 101, 102; and universities, 85-92, 100-101, 130-31, 135; and venture capital, 84-86, 88, 89, 90, 95-97, 99-100, 101. See also name of university or venture

New York Polytechnic Institute, 27, 66-67

New York (state), 66-67, 136-37

New York State Center for Advanced Technology (CAT). See Center for Advanced Technology

New York State Science and Technology Foundation, 53-54, 66

New York University, 81

Noranda, 16

Norris, William C., 71

North Carolina, University of, 63-64, 79

North Carolina A&T State University, 64

North Carolina Biotechnology Center, 65

North Carolina (state), 63-66

North Carolina State College, 79

North Carolina State University, 64. See also Research Triangle Park (Durham, North Carolina) Northeast Tier Advanced Technology Center (Lehigh University), 62

Northern Telecom, 64

Northrop, 45

Northwestern University, 26

OB/GYN Concepts Ltd., 82

Office of Technology Assessment, U.S. (OTA), 49, 54, 55, 118-24

Ohio University, 32

Olin Corporation, 43-44, 53

Optoelectronics, 76

Ornston, L. Nicholas, 42

Oxford University, 24

PacAmOr Bearings, 39

Paine Webber, 106, 107, 110

Patents: and corporate-university relationships, 23, 24, 25, 31, 32, 33; infringement of, 82, 83, 90; and international competition, 125; management of, 81-85; and new ventures, 88, 90, 100; and tax law changes, 88; and universities, 88, 90. See also University Patents, Inc.; name of specific university

Pennsylvania, University of, 62, 81

Pennsylvania Hospital (Philadelphia), 62

Pennsylvania Small Business Development centers, 63

Pennsylvania (state), 55, 61-63

Pennsylvania State University, 27, 62

Pennsylvania Technical Assistance program, 55

Peters, Lois, 21, 30-31, 103-4, 105-6, 110, 112

Pettingill, Gene, 65-66
Philips Signetics, 45
Pittsburgh, University of, 62
Plosila, Walter, 61, 63
Polymer Processing Program (MIT), 40
Princeton University, 81. *See also* Forrestal Center
Pro-competitive research, 71-80, 135
Product development, 8, 12, 13, 14, 16, 24, 30, 118, 124, 131
Product liability lawsuits, 90
PROSUS (Cornell Program on Submicrometer Structures), 36-37
Prudential Bache, 110
Ptashne, Mark, 46
Purdue University, 27, 50

R&D (research and development): corporate expenditures for, 2; Japanese–U.S. comparison of, 119-21; military, 116, 123; and scientific talent, 116-17; targeting of, 125; and tax laws, 124, 125; and venture companies, 120. *See also* R&D limited partnership; name of specific industry and country
R&D limited partnership: and biotechnology industry, 14-15, 19; and federal agencies/departments, 52, 75-76, 79-80, 125, 131; future of, 137-38; and new ventures, 95, 99-100, 102; and Software Productivity Consortium, 75. *See also* Corporate-university partnerships; Pro-competitive research
Regional Technology Development Organization Program (New York State), 67
Reimers, Niels, 91
Rensselaer Polytechnic Institute (RPI), 32, 37-39

Research Corporation, 42-43, 137
Research parks, 27-28, 32, 34-35, 39, 41, 43-44, 53, 132. *See also* name of specific park
Research Triangle Institute, 63, 64, 65
Research Triangle Park (Durham, North Carolina), 27, 63-64
Rhode Island, University of, 27
Richardson, John, 17
Risk taking: and biotechnology industry, 17, 19; and corporations, 8, 12, 79; government involvement in, 125; and new ventures, 89, 98, 99, 101; and universities, 89, 101
R. J. Reynolds Industries, 65
Rochester, University of, 27, 66-67
Rochester Polytechnic Institute, 39
Rockefeller University, 24
Rockwell International, 45
Root, Charles, 82
Rothschild, L. F., 108-9
Royalties: and corporate-university relationships, 23, 128; and MCC, 72; and new ventures, 83, 87, 89, 90, 93, 98, 99, 100; and technology transfer companies, 83, 84. *See also* Patents; Universities; name of specific venture organization
Rudman, Richard, 77
Rutgers University, 27, 50, 56, 77

Salk Institute, 27
San Diego, University of California at, 51
Santa Barbara, University of California at, 50
Saxonhouse, Gary, 119
Schumacher, Gebhard F. B., 82

Science and Technology Agency (New York State), 66
Scientific talent: and biotechnology industry, 7, 8-9, 11, 13-14, 19; competition for, 127-29; and corporation-university partnership, 21-22, 26, 127, 131-32; and federal government, 50, 136; Japanese, 116; and new ventures, 85-86, 96, 100; and pro-competitive research, 73-74, 76, 78, 80; R&D, 116-17; and state support, 55; and technology transfer companies, 93; and universities, 29-30, 32, 85-86, 127
Scripps Institute, 8, 26
Searle [G.D.] Corporation, 17, 24
Secrecy and corporate-university relationships, 23
Semiconductor industry, 22-23, 26, 35-36, 44-45, 72, 74. *See also* name of specific company or university
Semiconductor Research Corporation (SRC), 26, 35-36, 65, 73-75, 117, 135
Shareholders and pro-competitive research, 71, 73
Shewmaker, Bruce, 100
Sikorsky, 37
Small Business Innovation Development Act (1982), 52
Small Business Innovation Research program (NSF), 51-52, 84-85, 124
SmithKline Beckman, 82
Snyder, Ray, 33
Society of University Patent Administrators, 85
Software Productivity Consortium (SPC), 75, 80, 103
South Dakota, University of, 27
Sperry, 38

Stadler, George, 84
Stanford Industrial Park, 27
Stanford University, 16-17, 23, 26, 27, 32, 44-45, 90-91, 92
State government, 49, 54-55, 88, 134, 136-37. *See also* name of specific state
Steel companies, 79
Stockmarket and new ventures, 95, 97, 99, 101, 102
Stony Brook, State University of New York at, 66-67
Strategic Computing Program (U.S. government), 123
Submicron structures, 36-37
Subsidiaries. *See* Affiliates/subsidiaries
Sumney, Larry, 74-75
Sungene Technology, 18
Sun Oil Co., 106
Syracuse University, 66-67

Task Force on High Technology and Biotechnology (University of Maryland), 58-59
Task Force on Technological Innovation (National Governor's Association), 54-55
Tax laws, 50, 52-53, 88, 101, 124, 125, 130, 134, 136, 137-38
Technology centers. *See* name of specific center
Technology transfer companies, 82-84, 88, 92-93, 131-32, 137. *See also* New ventures; name of specific company
Technology transfers. *See* Biotechnology industry; Corporate-university partnerships; Technology transfer companies
Tektronix, 45
Television industry, 76-77
Temple University, 62

Texas, University of, 26
Texas A&M University, 27
Texas Instruments, 45
Thomas Edison program (Ohio), 88
Thomas Jefferson University, 62
Tianjin Cancer Institute (China), 14
TRW, 45, 64

Ulmer, Kevin, 59-60
Union Carbide, 33-34, 37, 64
United Kingdom, 115, 121-22, 123, 135
United Technologies, 37, 45
Universities: and commercialization, 134-35, 137; and conflict of interest, 85, 90-92, 93; and for-profit venture companies, 88-89, 91; German, 122-23; as initiator of corporate-university partnerships, 30; Japanese, 75, 121; levels of, 33; new ventures by, 85-92, 100-101, 130-31, 135; and patents, 31, 32, 33, 83-85, 88, 90; and pro-competitive research, 79; and risk taking, 89, 101; and state government, 88, 134; and theoretical knowledge, 29; and venture capital, 84-85, 86, 88, 89, 90, 101, 130. See also Scientific talent; name of university, venture organization, or technology transfer company
University City Science Center (Philadelphia), 43-44, 53, 62
University Communications, 81
University Genetics, 81
University Optical Products Co., 81, 83
University Patents, Inc., 81-84
University Technology, Inc., 87-89
UPI Research Corporation, 83-84
Urbana-Champaign, University of Illinois at, 51

Urban Development Action grants (HUD), 53
U.S. economy, corporate influence on, 1-5, 133. See also Competition
Utah, University of, 85-86
Utah Innovation Center, 86
Utterback, James, 39

Vanderbilt University, 79
Venture capital: availability of, 101; in California, 67; and federal support, 51-52; and high-technology business, 4, 7, 8-9, 19; and incubator concept, 34-35; Japanese, 119; and new ventures, 84-85, 86, 88, 89, 90, 95-97, 99-100, 101; and tax laws, 101; and technology transfer companies, 82; and universities, 84-85, 86, 88, 89, 90, 101, 130, 134. See also name of specific company or partnership

Wall, Michael, 14, 16
Warner-Lambert, 14
Washington University, 23-24, 90, 93, 131
Western Pennsylvania Advanced Technology Center (Carnegie-Mellon University and University of Pittsburgh), 62
West Germany, 2, 76, 115, 116, 122-23, 124, 135
Wolf, Edward, 36-37

Xerox, 38, 45
Xoma, 109

Yale University, 27, 41-44, 47, 53, 135
Young, J. Winslow, 85-86

About the Authors

ROBERT F. JOHNSTON, a leading venture capitalist, is President of
Johnston Associates Inc. and founder of six biotechnology companies.

CHRISTOPHER G. EDWARDS was founding Editor-in-Chief of
Bio/Technology magazine and is currently Director of Strategic Communications at Regis McKenna Inc., a marketing communications
consulting firm.